Home from the Hardware Store

Home from the Hardware Store

Transform Everyday Materials into Fabulous Home Furnishings

Stephen Antonson and Kathleen Hackett

Photographs by Lesley Unruh

RODALE

Rodale books may be purchased for business or promotional use or for special sales. For information, please write to: Special Markets Department, Rodale Inc., 733 Third Avenue, New York, NY 10017.

Printed in the United States of America

Rodale Inc. makes every effort to use acid-free ♾, recycled paper ♻.

Book design by Christina Gaugler

Photographs © 2010 by Lesley Unruh

Library of Congress Cataloging-in-Publication Data

Hackett, Kathleen.
 Home from the hardware store : transform everyday materials into fabulous home furnishings / Stephen Antonson and Kathleen Hackett ; photographs by Lesley Unruh.
   p.   cm.
 Includes index.
 ISBN-13 978–1–60529–572–5   paperback
 ISBN-10 1–60529–572–8   paperback
 1. House furnishings.   I. Antonson, Stephen.   II. Title.
TX311.H33 2010
747—dc22   2010026050

Distributed to the trade by Macmillan

2   4   6   8   10   9   7   5   3   1   paperback

RODALE
LIVE YOUR WHOLE LIFE™

We inspire and enable people to improve their lives and the world around them.

for Finn

&

James

CONTENTS

The Projects

The Instructions

"I love hardware stores and universities. Both offer an array of tools that reveal problems you didn't realize needed fixing until you went there."

—KEN GOLDBERG, UNIVERSITY PROFESSOR

"I like the smell, and the infinite variety in a small space, the experience of finding things you actually need that will solve real problems, unlike, say, shopping for clothes, where you end up spending a lot of money but not necessarily feeling any better off."

—TRISH HALL, EDITOR

"Its ability to inspire I would rate alongside the library and church."

—JOSEPH FRATESI, INDUSTRIAL DESIGNER

"Give me a wet afternoon and a trip to the hardware store and anything is possible."

—SARAH BUNE, INTERIOR DESIGNER

"The Dublin Hardware Store in Dublin, Michigan. I love this place. It's a hardware store/fishing and hunting outfitter/liquor store and grocery store in one. But their big thing is jerky. They make mountains of jerky for fishermen and hunters. When I'm in other countries, I always look for mousetraps in hardware stores. The variety and inventiveness is incredible."

—JOHN SCHWARZ, INDUSTRIAL DESIGNER

"Breakfast at the counter at Main Street Bistro in New Paltz followed by a trip to the True Value was my Sunday ritual for the nearly five years of fixing up my house. They once had a box of dental instruments at the counter—for like a buck apiece—perfect for stripping the tiny ogee and cove details of window and door frames. I never saw them there again, but they were the right thing at the right time, which is sort of the perfect metaphor for the hardware store experience."

—ANDREW GRAY, CREATIVE DIRECTOR

"They're the equivalent of a museum for ingenious inventions."

—JOSH MARGOLIS, MUSICIAN

"A hardware store is the ultimate laboratory for the creative mind."

—CARLO ALESSI, ARTIST/ENTREPRENEUR

"Mostly? I like the way they smell. It makes me feel nostalgic. Like I'm running an errand with my dad and we find the very specific bolt or nut that we need. And probably, we get some penny candy at the counter, too."

—LAUREN HOLDEN, CREATIVE STRATEGIST

"It's where you go when you know exactly what you need and when you don't know what you need."

—TAD HILLS, ARTIST AND AUTHOR

"Great hardware is always an enlightening transition from our body."

—MICHAEL GREY, ARTIST

INTRODUCTION

"Do something, do something to that, and then do something to that."

—JASPER JOHNS

In those twelve words, Jasper Johns provided our credo for *Home from the Hardware Store*. But the truth is, we'd been following the contemporary artist's simple directive ever since we've known each other (and individually, ever since we were born!).

It's been almost a decade since the day I mentioned in passing to Stephen that my apartment needed a chandelier. I was living in Paris at the time, and he had been logging a pile of miles on Air France. His night flight routinely landed just in time for us to head to Porte de Vanves, where one of Paris's renowned flea markets is held every Saturday. We spent hours there, seduced by the shapes, textures, and patinas (not to mention the fabulously eccentric vendors) that distinguish French flea markets from all others. The mere mention of a chandelier on one of those jaunts was all it took to set Stephen's left-brained wheels in motion and, while I was away at French class, he snuck off to the BHV.

Ahhhh, the BHV: Conjure up the dreamiest, quirkiest, most storied hardware store on earth, and you might hit upon an image of the Bazar de l'Hôtel de Ville. Stretched over hundreds of thousands of square feet, it offers everything you could possibly need to make, fix, or repair just about anything on earth. At this spectacular emporium, Stephen bought only a spool of baling wire, small chain, pliers, and a screw eye. Back in my tiny space, he fiddled with the wire, twisting, turning, clipping, and winding it until two hours later, when I returned to find a flickering *lumière* hanging over the dinner table. The room was transformed and I was transfixed. The rest, as they say, is history. You might say that Stephen had me at, well, baling wire.

Ten years later, we still consult the hardware store first—before the lighting shop, furniture store, or home boutique. Browsing there gives us the same adrenaline rush as treasure hunting in an antiques shop or eyeing the gleaming furniture at a specialty retailer might. If you think of this most utilitarian of places only as a store filled with objects expressly for keeping a home alive—nails to connect a joint, polystyrene to warm the walls—then it's time to look at it again. Actually, it's time to look at it as if you're seeing it for the first time. The best hardware stores are crammed with personality, and that doesn't necessarily mean the customers or the department managers are (though it certainly can!). The characters are on the shelves: the type-A pegboard, the flashy copper roofing, the mysterious matte insulation. When you hit the hardware store *just to look around and see what's there*, the HVAC pieces, piping, tubing, and rope begin to register as shapes, textures, and finishes rather than as heating and cooling systems, plumbing parts, or ductwork.

Indeed, Alexander Calder sums up our guiding design principle. "I paint with shapes," he famously said. As in a beginner's drawing course, start with lines, circles, squares, and rectangles, and go from there. Forget that cylindrical concrete molds are used to pour foundations; the tubes make for great storage. Chop one up, cover the pieces with decorative paper, and hang them, grouped together, on the wall. Ignore the fact that plumbing bushings are supposed to connect pipes; screw the graduated connectors into one another to make handsome candlesticks. Mason line may not bring out the bricklayer in you, but when wrapped around a drab lamp base, the bleached cotton rope's soft hue and organic texture are transformative. And that reflective insulation? There's no better material for swiftly turning a 6-year-old into a knight in shining armor.

The infinite variety. The smell. The paint-shaker-in-the-back-of-the-store sound. Nostalgia plays a big role in the lure of the hardware store. Our hope is that as you turn the following pages, you'll begin to see the place anew—and with that, the promise it holds for creating lovely things for your home.

The
Projects

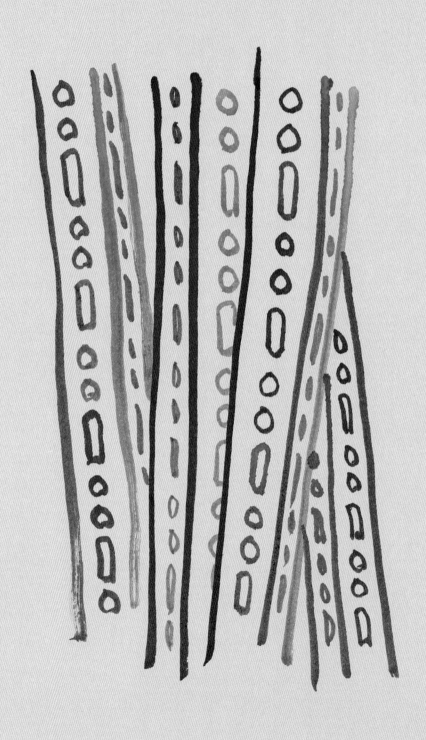

1

Seven Important Pieces

"Design addresses itself to the need," said Charles Eames, one half of one of the 20th century's foremost design duos. He and his wife, Ray, espoused a philosophy—good design at minimal cost with prefabricated parts—that we adopted as we surveyed the hardware store for the furniture ideas in this chapter. Whether we needed the pieces that follow or not, they compel us for the same reasons the Eameses turned plywood into their iconic lounge chair.

PEGBOARD + PINE
STOCK = GRAPHIC
PEDESTAL
(see page 63)
*Pegboard's utilitarian
quality has long been
known to us, but its grid
of dots is what drew us
to this unexpected use—
a sleek and minimalist
pedestal appropriate for
a cherished sculpture,
your children's art, or a
bust of Beethoven.*

In the plumbing aisle, there is galvanized ductwork that when connected to form rings, stacked like doughnuts, and then topped with a round piece of pine makes a one-of-a-kind table. A pair of hollow-core doors, the bane of interior designers, covered with protective floor paper and embellished with thumbtacks becomes a folding screen that any David Hicks devotee would love. And then there are the steel supports in the shelving aisle. Bolted together, they make chic industrial frames for tables or chairs; plywood and pine boards supply the sitting and eating surfaces.

SAWHORSES + MDF +
CANVAS DROP CLOTH
= CHIC WORK TABLE
(see page 66)
*"Only a #9 brass head
will do," Dorothy Draper
was fond of saying.
With all due respect to
the beloved mid-20th-
century decorator, we
used cut tacks here,
inspired by Paris flea
market canvases, which
are always held to their
stretchers with these.*

The Eameses' "most of the best to the greatest number for the least" credo notwithstanding, our hope is that the pieces here inspire you to see common items—plumbing parts, pegboard, and luan doors—primarily as shapes, patterns, and textures. When you do, the possibility for original designs is endless.

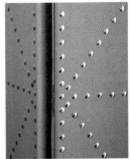

KRAFT PAPER + LUAN BIFOLD DOORS = FABULOUS FOLDING SCREEN (see page 70) *Inspired by a pair of leather upholstered doors designed by Jean-Michel Frank, the French designer known for his minimalist interiors, we saw potential in a roll of reinforced kraft paper (it protects floors during a renovation) and a bulk supply of thumbtacks.*

CEMENT BOARD + FOUND FURNITURE = PARCHMENT-TOP TABLE (see page 76) *To achieve the look and warmth of parchment, head over to the flooring aisle and stop in front of the cement board, a material typically used as a substrate for tiled floors or walls. Naked, it resembles a natural material; our first thought was limestone. With a coat of shellac, though, it becomes something else altogether.*

SHELF SUPPORTS + WIDE PINE BOARDS = SNAP-TOGETHER FARM TABLE (see page 73) *If you look at shelf supports as you would a child's Erector set, you'll see that they present as many design possibilities as the classic building toy. Bolted together into a rectangle, the L-shaped pieces form a rim for the pine board top to rest on. Their L shape also allows them to become legs that provide enough support to hold the whole thing up.*

Andy Warhol   Drawings 1942 – 1987

GALVANIZED ELBOWS + PAINTED TABLETOP = SPACE-AGE COFFEE
TABLE (see page 78) *If Marc Newson's Lockheed Lounge chair, which
recently sold at auction for over $1 million, is out of reach, perhaps a few
galvanized elbows will satisfy. Drawn to their arced shape, ribbed
pattern, and shine, we found the tubes just begging to be stacked and
attached, Michelin Man–style, into a perfect pedestal for a coffee table.*

SHELF SUPPORTS +
PLYWOOD = TWO-
HOUR CHAIR (see
page 82) *It's child's play,
really. If your attention
span rivals the 8-and-
under set, then there's
nothing like a few strips
of steel, some nuts and
bolts, and a sheet of
plywood to hook you
into making this
sculptural chair.*

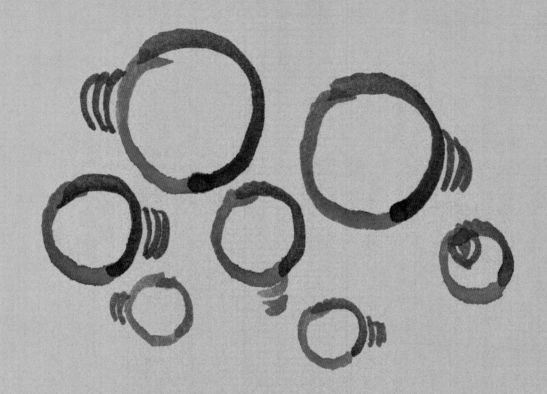

2

Everything
Is
Illuminated

When Benjamin Franklin wrote, "I am much in the dark about light," he wasn't referring to picking out a pair of sconces or choosing the right desk lamp. But his sentiment does resonate with anyone who has ever had to pick out lighting—the designs are countless, the options endless, and the quality ranges from throwaway to pedigreed.

In our New York City neighborhood, the night before trash pickup tells the story best. Broken floor-style torchiere lamps are as plentiful as trash barrels. It makes

DRAIN GRATES + LAMP KIT = CONSTRUCTIVIST LAMP (see page 90) *You'd never guess that this lamp is made with plastic drain grates from the plumbing section. Looking past their tennis court green color, we saw a great graphic pattern that only gets better when the grates are stacked. The matte black paint gives the illusion that they are made of metal.*

sense, this glut of cheaply made lighting, since all you really need to create it is a cord, socket, and bulb. And that's where the hardware store comes in. If you have the ability to screw in a lightbulb, you can make the most playful—and high-quality—lights in this chapter. There's even one that takes exactly five minutes to put together with just your hands—and it will never fail you.

(continued on page 18)

BAR CLAMP + CLAMP LIGHT = FIVE-MINUTE DESK LAMP (see page 93) *Stephen's brother, an artist, gets credit for this ingenious lamp, a clever example of necessity being the mother of invention. On the day he moved into his studio, he needed a quick light source and, pulling together what was on hand, the Five-Minute Desk Lamp was born.*

BALING WIRE + CHAIN = MRS.
ASTOR'S CHANDELIER (see page 94)
*There's nothing like a chandelier
to lend a space a little je ne sais
quoi. Admittedly, choosing one can
be as big a commitment as deciding
on a sofa, but when it's made
from inexpensive wire and chain,
you can relax a little.*

Drum Shade + Rug Pad = Honeycomb Lamp Shade (see page 100)
We pulled the pad right out from under the rug, so to speak, and wrapped it around a plain white drum shade to surprisingly cool effect. The white-on-white looks especially beautiful when the light is turned on.

COTTON MASON LINE + STOCK LAMP = ROPE-WRAPPED LAMP (see page 86) *Most of the lamps in the hardware store are underwhelming, if not downright unattractive. But if you can look beyond their ugly finishes and to their shapes, there is possibility—especially if you cover them up. We wrapped these with cotton mason line.*

We have long been drawn to beautiful lighting. To our minds, it's the most important design element in a room. Our approach, to both the fixture itself and the light it throws, is sculptural, which makes the hardware store a terrific resource for designing your own. Pick up a ductwork cap in the heating and cooling aisle and envision it clipped onto a lightbulb. A jet-black piece of woodstove pipe, arched just so, makes a wonderful "shade" for decorative lights arranged here and there on a bookcase. Even a lamp with a great shape but an unappealing finish has possibilities—especially if you wrap it in cotton rope.

Our passion for great lighting has a lot to do with its ability to transform a room with no more effort than the flick of a switch or the strike of a match. The plumbing section provides us with perhaps our most inspired idea: candlesticks and a candelabrum constructed from graduated pipe fittings. If only Mr. Franklin had had the opportunity to stroll through a hardware store. We're sure he would have found it illuminating.

CRIMP ELBOW +
PLEXIGLAS =
PERISCOPE LAMP
(see page 102) *The shape
of this coal black
elbow—familiar to you
if you grew up in a
home heated by a
woodstove—looked to us
like a version of Italian
designer Elio
Martinelli's 1960s
cantilevered table light.*

Plumbing Parts + Elbow Grease = Instant Candelabrum (see page 104)
Steel plumbing pipes and fittings are the Lincoln Logs of the hardware store; they're so enticing that we found ourselves clearing off shelf space in the aisle so we'd have room to play with them. It didn't take long for us to realize that incorporating pipes into this design had us seeing "plumbing" and not "beautiful candelabrum," so we used only the fittings, to much more appealing effect.

PLUMBING PARTS + ELBOW GREASE =
MACHINE-AGE CANDLESTICKS
(see page 106) *Easy enough for a child to
screw together, these handsome
candlesticks require no more talent or
knowledge than this: Righty, tighty; lefty,
loosey. You screw them together. That's it!*

DUCTWORK + BULB
ADAPTER = ODE TO
GIACOMETTI WALL
SCONCE (see page 88)
*Before becoming a
world-famous sculptor,
Alberto Giacometti
teamed up with designer
Jean-Michel Frank to
create light fixtures,
lamps, fireplace
surrounds, and
hardware. This duct-
work cap, painted white
and fitted out with a
bulb clip, recalls one of
the pendant lights that
came out of that
collaboration.*

ADAPTERS + BULBS = MOLECULAR DESK LIGHT (see page 89) *This design-as-you-go lamp was highly influenced by our experiences in seventh grade science lab, where we built molecules out of wooden sticks and balls.*

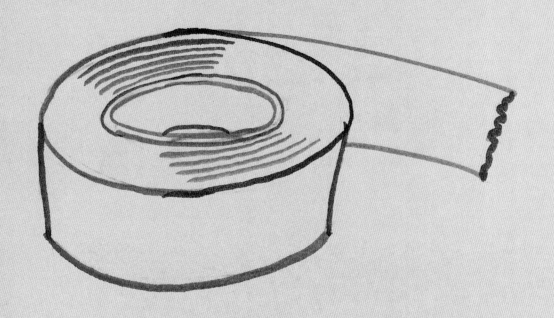

3

If These Walls Could Talk

This chapter is for those who mistakenly believe that the only choices for beautifying walls are a bucket of paint or a few rolls of wallpaper. Indeed, a coat of gorgeous high-gloss or a striking print can dramatically change the vibe of a room, but limiting yourself to the paint section means that you're not seeing all of the possibilities. Glossy strips of aluminum tape, for example, vertically adhered to the wall, deliver the kind of glamour one doesn't usually associate with the hardware store. Likewise, cut pieces of screen molding affixed to

walls in square and rectangular shapes mimic the wood-carved look of the beautiful boiseries in so many Paris apartments.

Transforming an existing wall is one thing, but creating one where there is none pushed us to think vertically. Sometimes the answer lies in simply changing a product's orientation. We picked up molds used to lay down a "stone" patio and suspended a group of them from the ceiling to make a transparent wall. Similarly, we took a drop cloth off the floor, installed it in a ceiling-mounted track, and created a soft, flexible, floor-to-ceiling curtain perfect for separating space in a room such as a bedroom with an office. Think vertically. That's the only requirement when creating walls.

FOIL TAPE + A BLAND WALL = STERLING STRIPED WALLPAPER (see page 108) *A few rolls of reflective tape later, our dining room went from a basic gray to glamorous.*

CORK TILE + WOOD GLUE = SOFT-TOUCH SWITCH PLATE (see page 110) *If we had time, we'd carve our switch plates from wood, the way influential sculptor and wood craftsman Wharton Esherick did. After all, we use switches every day, and touching a nature-made material beats putting fingertips to plastic any day.*

COUNTRY STONE MOLD + STOVE BOLTS = LACY ROOM DIVIDER (see page 112) *Sometimes you have to simply change a material's orientation to see its potential. Pick up one of these plastic molds, attach several of them to one another, and hang them vertically to create a fantastic patterned "wall" that's ideal for a loft space.*

Canvas Drop Cloth + Hospital Tracking + Paint = "Wall" of Frames (see page 117) *Drop cloths have wonderful heft and weave, making them great for upholstering chairs and sofas, unfurling onto a table (see page 128), hanging as floor-length curtains, or creating a soft, sliding wall as we did here. Fornasetti supplied the inspiration for the painted frames.*

STOCK MOLDING + PAINT
= FAUX BOISERIE (see
page 115) Some walls need
embellishing beyond the
baseboard. Rather than
covering them entirely with
wood paneling, make it look
like you did with a bit of
chair rail and screen
molding.

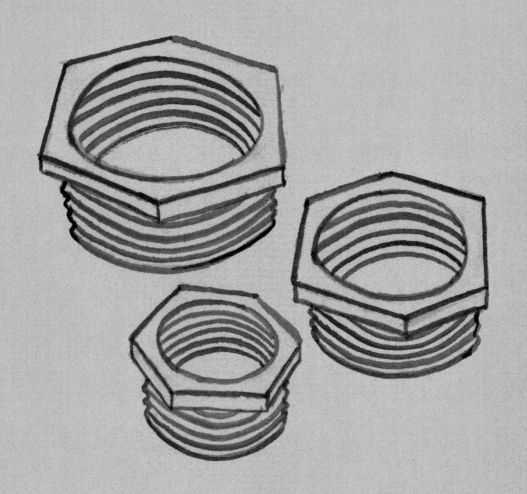

4

Details, Details

Forget function. Everything in a hardware store has one, but that's not the point here. In fact, it's to your advantage if you haven't a clue what wye tubes, screw posts, or rolls of copper flashing are supposed to do. What does matter is having that "aha!" moment—the idea that springs forth when you look straight past the intended use of something and you see its shape or texture. Combine that with a bit of playfulness, and the hardware store becomes a place full of decorative parts just begging to be cleverly put together.

Take copper flashing. Not only is its warm glow irresistible, but it comes on a roll the width of a table runner. Notice that, and the lightbulb goes on. The wye tube? Forget you're in the plumbing department; this jaunty piece of PVC brings to mind the iconic shape of a Giacometti vase, albeit a tongue-in-cheek version.

(continued on page 39)

TACKS + PLYWOOD = FOLK ART FAMILY SILHOUETTES (see page 120) *Purists might take issue with our silhouettes, which traditionally don't have an eye and do have razor-sharp contours. Because we're outlining the shape with cut tacks, the lines here are softer, leaving you to fill in the rest with your eyes.*

VINYL NUMBERS + PROTECTIVE PADS = CHAIN-LINK MIRROR FRAME (see page 122) *You don't have to know how to draw or paint to embellish a plain mirror frame. Overlap a bunch of adhesive vinyl zeroes from the hardware store (you'll find them near the locks), and they turn into a chain-link pattern.*

PVC TUBE = FAUX 40s
MOD VASE (see page 124)
*This Y-shaped tube
recalls the lines of a very
rare 1940s French
plaster vase. Fill it with
limber-stemmed flowers
and frothy blooms, such
as these ranunculus,
which seem to share the
same sense of humor as
the vase itself.*

INSULATION + BLUNT WRITING TOOL = OPEN GUEST BOOK (see
page 126) *This framed piece of insulation first hung in our dining room,
where it was curiously beautiful when illuminated by candlelight. After a
friend took the blunt end of a pen to it, we hung it in the hallway, where
guests now sign their names—or become their alter egos. (Apparently,
Marcel Duchamp has been over for dinner.)*

DENIM DROP CLOTH =
DROP-DEAD GOR-
GEOUS TABLECLOTH
(see page 128) *Just like a
great pair of jeans, this
tablecloth can go casual
or formal, depending on
what you set on top of it.
We throw it over our
table wrong side up
because we prefer the
lighter color and subtle
weave.*

And if a screw post, the sophisticated cousin of a nut and bolt, is designed to give furniture a finished look, why not use a pair to fasten the French cuffs on a man's shirt? We like to call it the Lampshade Principle—it just makes sense that some people are compelled to put one on their head.

SCREW POSTS +
FRENCH CUFFED
SHIRT = CLEVER CUFF
LINKS (see page 125) *Screw posts are used in
place of a nut, bolt, and
washer to give the
exposed hardware on
furnishings a finished
look. Here, they do the
same on Stephen's
French cuff shirt.*

Sliding Pads + Paint = Pointillist Silhouette (see page 132) *If driving tacks into a board isn't your cup of tea (see page 120), you might find the gentler approach of sticking dots on canvas a more pleasant method for making a silhouette.*

ROPE + PINE BOARD = NAME-DROPPING WALL ART (see page 130) *Kids love to see their names written large, but it's especially magical when the letters are shaped out of rope—a material they find only useful for jumping or tying things together.*

COPPER BASKETS –
THEIR HANDLES =
MODERNIST WALL
DISPLAY (see page 134)
*Donald Judd is
synonymous with
minimalism, though it
is a description he never
liked. He wanted his
work to reference itself
and the space around
it—a principle that
inspired the use of these
simple copper boxes as
wall sculpture.*

COPPER FLASHING + BLUNT TOOL =
ARTS AND CRAFTS TABLE RUNNER
(see page 136) *Unfurled on the dining
room table, copper flashing makes a
beautiful runner, especially for dinner
by candlelight. A bit of embossing or
debossing, easily done with the blunt
end of a paintbrush or dull pencil,
intensifies its beauty.*

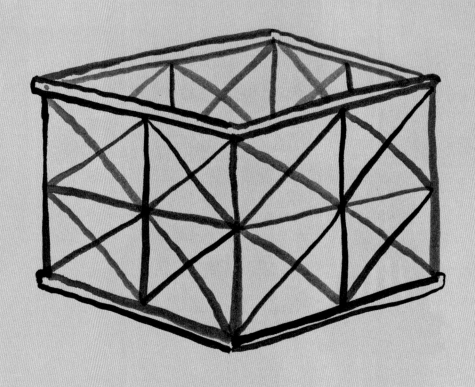

5

Putting It Away

We have a dear and talented friend who always seems to have everything in the right place—organized, ordered, and labeled. He swears that to find appropriate storage, you must look everywhere *but* the stores devoted to it. Not only is there not much beauty in their products, but the offerings are pretty much one size fits all, too.

For us, that alternative source is the hardware store. And to keep our wits about us, we set a rule for ourselves when it comes to designing useful storage: The ideas either have to improve upon an existing storage

PEGBOARD + COLOR-
FUL RUBBER BANDS =
NO-THUMBTACK
BULLETIN BOARD (see
page 139) *This alterna-
tive to a traditional
bulletin board lets you
"tack up" 3-D objects.
It's an especially great
option in a child's room,
where stray tacks can
find their way into
little feet.*

item or simplify it. A fistful of rubber bands strung on a pegboard allows you to "pin" three-dimensional objects to it. The lowly plastic stacking crate, painted matte white and topped with a painted piece of Plexiglas, makes a slick bedside table—with storage space inside for books and magazines. Plumbing parts like flanges, nipples, and elbows—screwed together and onto pine boards and then stacked— make a shelving unit that's about as simple as it gets, and with a

(continued on page 50)

CORK TILES + WOOD
GLUE = FOOLPROOF
ORGANIZER (see
page 142) *Cork has a
gripping quality, so it's
a great material for
making a landing spot
for your keys, glasses,
and wallet. The beauty
of this organizer is that
it instantly clues you in
if you're about to walk
out the door without,
well, your wallet
or keys.*

FLOOR FLANGES +
THREADED PIPES +
PINE BOARDS =
QUICK-ASSEMBLY
SHELVES (see page 148)
*If you can thread a nut
onto a bolt, you can put
together these sturdy
shelves. There's no
building expertise
involved, apart from
using a hand drill to
fasten the supports to
the boards.*

PLASTIC CRATE + PLEXIGLAS = SEE-THROUGH STORAGE
(see page 150) *With a few coats of white paint, the storage bins favored by college kids everywhere become sleek white cubes with a porcelainlike finish.*

raw, unembellished beauty that could never be duplicated with materials from anywhere but the hardware store.

Unlike the decorative pieces in the previous chapter, the shelves, tubes, and boxes here are nothing if not functional. However, they are all designed to reside out in the open, not behind closed doors. Some of them are sculptural objects in their own right. Tubular building forms, chopped into varying heights and bolted together in a biomorphic shape, bring life to a wall, whether empty or stacked with hats, gloves, and mittens. The real beauty of these mod "shelves" is that, like a living thing, they can grow. Great storage doesn't get any better than that.

CARDBOARD BUILDING FORMS + CONTACT PAPER = MODULAR STORAGE (see page 144) *What storage unit could be better than one that grows with your needs? These tubes are used to form concrete posts during building construction, but turn them on their sides and they make a wonderful amorphous pattern— perfect for hanging on the wall.*

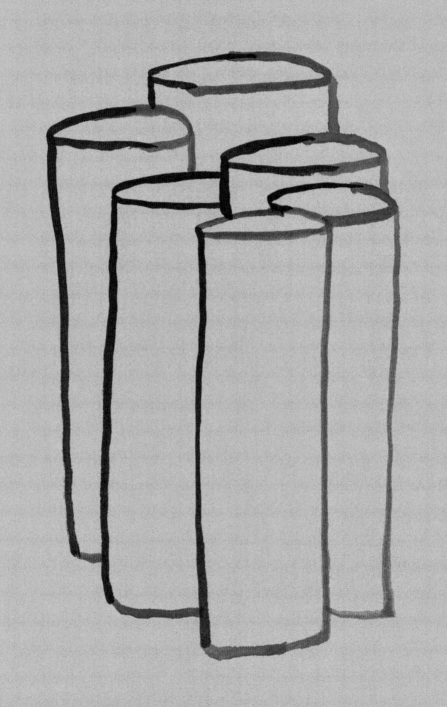

6

Child's Play

Excuse the expression, but we really *are* like kids in a candy store in any place that sells hardware. But there's nothing like the knee-high set to bring out the playful side of paint cans, pulleys, and plumbing parts. In fact, bringing children along on a trip to the hardware store guarantees free design inspiration. What 4-year-old can resist pulling on a spool of colorful rope? (Or on *every single spool* of colorful rope?) To young eyes, a dowel looks like a sword handle, a round piece of pine is a wheel, and shiny insulation might as well be a knight's armor.

BUILDING FORMS + PLUMBING PARTS + DUCTWORK = ROYAL ROBOT FLOOR LAMP (see page 156) *Inspired by one of Stephen's fondest memories, this version of a robot is decidedly more tricked out than the one his dad built him from boxes (for the body) and a round ice cream tub (for the head). Both featured what he still remembers as the pièce de résistance—a doorbell belly button.*

Our two young boys are behind the projects on these pages, but admittedly, some recall fond childhood memories of our own. Making a fort under a table apparently still ranks high on the fun meter, all these decades later. So does having a robot in your room, especially if it lights up and has a doorbell belly button. To our great surprise, the age-old game of ringtoss still compels, likely because we crafted one from hot yellow, bright pink, and Yves Klein blue parts.

(continued on page 59)

PAINT CAN + PULLEY + ROPE = BUCKET OF FUN (see page 163) *Two boys, one top bunk. Our solution to the endless discussion of who sleeps on top was to give the boy down below control over what goes into the "top secret" bucket.*

NYLON ROPE + MASON LINE = RINGTOSS REDUX (see page 152)
There's no ignoring the retina-scorching color of mason line in the rope
and twine aisle. Wrapped around blazing yellow rope, it's a no-fail way
to brighten a child's day.

ROLLER SHADES + PERMANENT MARKER = KIDS'
CLUBHOUSE (see page 154) *Where do kids always end up
after Thanksgiving dinner? We took the table-as-fort idea
one step further. By installing a few simple roller shades
along the table's apron, we encourage hiding out under the
dining room table!*

BUILDING FORMS + SOLID PINE ROUNDS = QUIET CANNON (see page 164) *With a costume box filled to overflowing, dress up is big around our house. Nothing in that chest gets more play than a pair of tricorn hats, souvenirs from a visit to Monticello. The only thing missing was the cannon—until we put a pair of pine rounds together with a cardboard tube painted matte black.*

Whether there are children in the picture or not, the ideas on these pages are worth a good look. They exemplify the unrestrained imagination of a child. And, as Picasso said, "Every child is an artist. The problem is how to remain an artist once we grow up."

INSULATION + VELCRO = SNAP-ON SUIT OF ARMOR (see page 168) *In addition to being metallic, the insulation used here features a pattern reminiscent of chain mail. This is the basic suit—add on shoe covers, a belt, and a sword or spear for the deluxe model!*

THE
INSTRUCTIONS

1

Furniture

Graphic Pedestal

The $^3/_{16}$-inch-thick white pegboard used here is available in 4×8-foot sheets. If you don't have your own table saw, have the sheets cut to size right at the hardware store.

MATERIALS

2 pieces white pegboard, $34" \times 12" \times {}^3/_{16}"$ each

2 pieces white pegboard, $34" \times 11^5/_8" \times {}^3/_{16}"$ each

1 piece white pegboard, $12" \times 12" \times {}^3/_{16}"$

4 pieces hardwood millwork, $34" \times 1" \times 1"$ each

4 pieces hardwood millwork, $9^5/_8" \times 1" \times 1"$ each

40 #6 wood screws, 1" long, each colored on the head with a black marker

TOOLS

Table saw

Handsaw

Black permanent marker

Wood glue

Drill with a Phillips-head bit

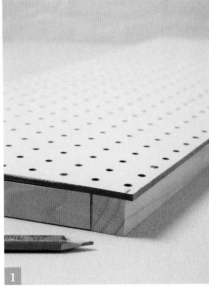
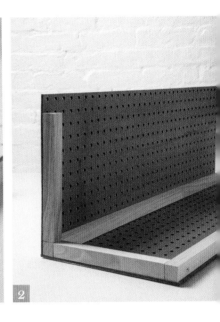

1. On a clean work surface, place one 34" × 12" piece of pegboard right side up. On each 12" end, measure and use a pencil to lightly mark ³⁄₁₆" in from the corners. Place two of the 34" lengths of millwork on the work surface parallel to each other and about 12" apart. Run a bead of wood glue down the center of each piece. Set the marked pegboard right side up on top of the millwork, allowing the pegboard to overhang by ³⁄₁₆" on either side. (Use the marks on the pegboard as guides.) Use a drill with a Phillips-head bit to screw the pegboard to the wood from the top, placing a screw at the fourth hole from each edge and one screw in the center. Run a bead of wood glue along one side of a piece of 9⅝"-long millwork. Slide it between the attached pieces of millwork on one end, aligning it so that it is flush with the attached pieces. Screw it to the pegboard from the top, placing one screw in the third hole from each end. Repeat with the remaining 34" × 12" piece of pegboard.

2. Lay one 34" × 11⅝" piece of pegboard right side up on the work surface. On one short end, measure and mark 1" in from both corners. Run a bead of wood glue along one side of a piece of 9⅝"-long millwork. Set the short edge of the pegboard on it, using the marks as guides and aligning it so that the top edges are flush with the short end of the board. Screw it to the pegboard from the front, placing one screw three holes in from each end. Repeat with the second 34" × 11⅝" board.

Lay one framed-out 34" × 12" piece of pegboard wrong side up on the work surface. Run a bead of wood glue along the length of the outside edge of the millwork. Position one 34" × 11⅝" piece of pegboard at a right angle to it, aligning the millwork at the top so that it is flush. Screw the pieces together from the front of the pegboard, placing one screw five holes in from each end and one screw in the center.

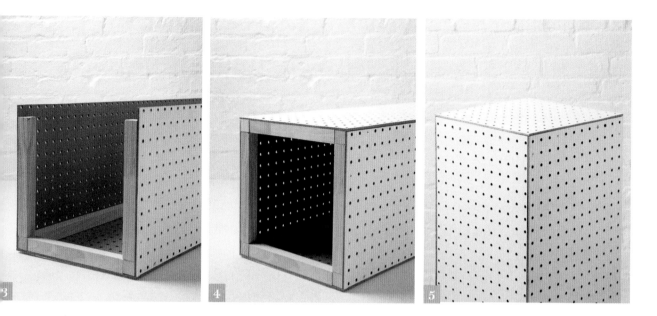

3. Repeat as above with the remaining 34" × 11⅝" piece of pegboard.

4. Run a bead of wood glue along the length of the outside edge of the millwork on the vertical pieces of pegboard. Screw the remaining 34" × 12" piece of pegboard to the pedestal from the front of the board, placing a screw in the fourth hole from each end and one screw in the center.

5. Stand the pedestal upright, with the millwork frame at the top, and run a bead of wood glue around the center of the frame. Place the 12"-square piece of pegboard on top, aligning its edges with the sides of the pedestal. Screw the top to the base, placing screws three holes in from each corner.

Chic Work Table

It's hard to find good-looking sawhorses today; most are plastic and unattractive. The beauty of these sawhorses is twofold: They're good looking *and* they're adjustable.

The brackets are designed to accommodate wooden legs of whatever length you choose, making them wonderfully versatile. You can design a desk-height piece or, if you prefer to stand while working on your projects, one that's a bit taller. The instructions below are for a tabletop that is 28 inches high.

Two-by-fours come in 8-foot lengths, so if you're cutting them yourself, you'll need three of them for this project. You can save yourself that step by asking the guy in the lumber department to cut them for you.

The desktop is made from medium-density fiberboard (MDF) covered with a cotton canvas drop cloth. The canvas has a bit of give, so the trick is to pull it just taut enough to achieve a smooth surface, but not so tight that it puckers. A coat of primer and paint makes it easy to wipe away spills and helps prevent staining. (Applying them is not a necessary step, but it does seal the fabric without masking the weave of the cotton.) Traditional upholstery tacks are stocked in the same section as the irregularly cut variety we use here.

Clean the desktop as you would any painted surface—use a damp cloth. If the stain is stubborn, just paint over it!

MATERIALS

16' × 9' canvas drop cloth

6 8½" × 33" × ¾" sheet medium-density fiberboard (MDF)

⅜" heavy-duty staples

1 quart primer

1 quart semigloss paint for the top (we used Benjamin Moore Grant Beige/HC #83)

1 quart semigloss paint for the legs and braces (we used Benjamin Moore China White 1-74)

1 package (2 ounces) #6 × ½" cut tacks

8 pine two-by-fours, 25" long each

2 pine two-by-fours, 29" long each

2 pairs sawhorse brackets

48 nails, #8d 1½"

TOOLS

Staple gun

220-grit sandpaper

120-grit sandpaper

Chop saw

2" all-paints paintbrush

Hammer

1. Cut the drop cloth into a 74½" × 39" rectangle (the dimensions of the tabletop plus 3" on all sides). Spread the drop cloth on a clean, flat surface and center the MDF on top of it. Beginning with one short side, staple the drop cloth to the back of the MDF, beginning in the middle of the short side and working to the right and then the left. Tug the cloth firmly, but not too much, to prevent any creases from forming on the desktop. Staple the opposite end of the table in the same manner, then do the long sides of the table. Make smooth corners by tucking the fabric in on itself so that it is parallel with the edges of the table.

2. Turn the tabletop right side up. Prime, sand with the 220-grit sandpaper, and paint the top and sides. Measure and use a pencil to lightly mark the center of the outside edge of the table every few inches, and connect the marks lightly to make a straight line around the entire perimeter. Make a light pencil mark every ½" along the line. Tap the cut tacks into each mark with a hammer. Erase the pencil marks in between.

3. Sand all surfaces of the cut two-by-fours with 120-grit sandpaper. Prime them and let them dry. Sand a second time with the 220-grit sandpaper. Wipe down every two-by-four with a soft cloth to remove any debris. Place the legs and rails on a clean work surface. Paint three sides and the cut ends of the legs and rails and let them dry. When they're dry, flip them over and paint the remaining bare sides. Let them dry.

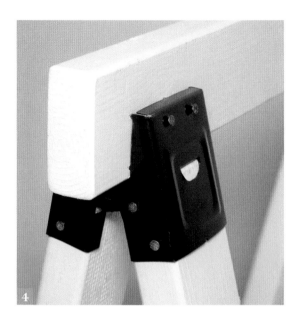

4. To assemble the table, insert the 25"
two-by-fours into the brackets up to the metal
stop, following the package directions. Hammer nails through the holes on both sides of the
brackets. Insert a 29" two-by-four (a rail) into
a bracket. Spread the legs until the teeth in
the bracket penetrate the rail. Secure the rail by
hammering nails through the holes in the top of
the bracket. Repeat on the other end. Repeat
with the second pair of brackets.

5. The sawhorses should be positioned so that
the tabletop overhangs the bottom of the outer
legs by 3". Arrange the sawhorses where you
want to put your table, then have a friend help
you lift the tabletop onto them.

Fabulous Folding Screen

Reinforced kraft paper is used for protecting floors during a renovation. It has a fiberglass weave that strengthens it, which is an advantage when you're adhering it to these doors. The paper has a right and a wrong side, with the fiberglass threads showing through more prominently on the wrong side. We used this "wrong side" as the right side on the panel, simply because we liked the texture it added. Standard-grade kraft paper will work in place of the reinforced kind, but it is not as forgiving and can tear easily as the adhesive sets.

Luan panels have a wood frame on their long edges, making it a challenge to push thumbtacks into these sides without prepping the holes with an awl and hammer first. The interior of the panels, on the other hand, is hollow, so this part of the project will go quickly without any prep work.

You'll need a roomy workspace to make this screen—the doors are almost 7 feet long.

MATERIALS

2 bifold luan doors, 79" × 30"

1 quart latex primer

1 quart semigloss latex paint

1 roll painter's tape, 1½" wide

1 roll reinforced kraft paper,
  300' × 36"

3M Super 77 Multipurpose
  Adhesive

1,000 nickel thumbtacks, $^{13}/_{32}$"

2 utility hinges, 2½"

8 vinyl-base nail-on glides, 4" × ¾"

TOOLS

2" all-paints paintbrush

Very sharp scissors

Utility knife with very sharp blades

Steel measuring tape

Straight edge

Awl

Tack hammer

Cordless drill with a Phillips-head bit

1. Prime and paint the backs of the doors in your desired color and let them dry thoroughly. Place one set of bifold doors, front side up, on the edge of a work surface so that one half is horizontal and the other hangs over the edge at the hinge. Affix the painter's tape along the horizontal edge of the hanging door to protect it from the adhesive.

2. Cut two 7'-long pieces of kraft paper and fold them in half lengthwise, making sharp creases. With a sharp pair of scissors, cut along each crease. Following the directions on the adhesive, spray it onto the face and two long edges of the door set on your work surface. Center one piece of the kraft paper on the door, wrong side up, and smooth it with your hands. Press firmly to remove any bubbles. Fold the kraft paper over the door's long edges, making a sharp crease at each corner. Use a utility knife to trim away excess paper where it meets the back edge of the door, then fold the door flat to trim away the excess paper on the inside edge. Remove the tape from the other half of the door and cover it in the same way. Set this set of doors aside, and repeat on the second bifold door.

3. Place one bifold door right side up on a work surface to sketch the design for the thumbtacks. Measure and lightly mark each door $3/8$" from the long edges, 2" from one of the short edges, and 1" from the opposite short edge. (The end with the 2" border will be the bottom of the screen.) Measure and mark horizontal lines every 19" from one of the lines along a short edge. Measure and mark the center of each rectangle. On the rectangles, along the top and bottom of the screen, draw a line from one corner of the rectangle, through the center, and to the opposite corner. Repeat, beginning at the other corner. Mark along all of the lines at 1" intervals. Repeat on the other door. On the middle sections of the screens, draw a line from one corner, through the midpoint, and to the opposite corner, following the design in the photo.

4. Along the long sides of each door, use an awl and tack hammer to make tiny pilot holes at the 1" intervals you marked. Along the top, bottom, and interior, use both hands and hold the awl at a slight angle as you very gently press the awl into the marks, just to make an impression. Do not press too hard or the awl will go through the luan and the tacks won't hold. (See Nuts and Bolts on this page.) Using the tack hammer, gently tap the thumbtacks into the luan at the marked intervals, pressing them with your thumb until they are flush with the surface.

5. Lay the screens side by side and facedown on a clean work surface. Align the hinges with the preinstalled hinges on each bifold door,

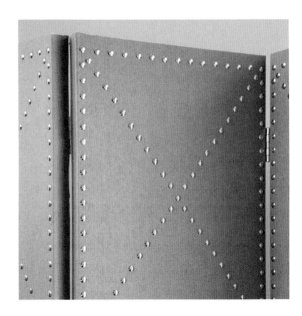

positioning them so that the barrel faces the front of the screen. Use an awl to make pilot holes in the screens where the holes in the hinges are. Fasten the hinges to the screens with a drill with a Phillips-head bit.

6. Hammer two vinyl glides to the bottom of each section of each door, placing them about $3/4$" from each edge.

Nuts and Bolts

If the Thumbtack Doesn't Fit . . .

If you make a hole—rather than an impression—in the luan with the awl, there's a good chance a thumbtack won't hold. All is not lost, however. Simply apply a bit of school glue to the shaft of the thumbtack, insert it into the hole, and let dry.

Snap-Together Farm Table

Shelf supports have alternating pairs of round and elliptical holes. The round holes are $\frac{3}{8}$ inch wide—a bit larger than the bolts we used. This is deliberate; it gives you a little wiggle room in order to get the corners perfectly square.

MATERIALS

2 plated steel slotted angle shelf supports,
   $6' \times 1\frac{1}{2}" \times 1\frac{1}{2}"$ each

2 plated steel slotted angle shelf supports,
   $3' \times 1\frac{1}{2}" \times 1\frac{1}{2}"$ each

4 plated steel slotted angle shelf supports,
   $3' \times 2\frac{1}{4}" \times 1\frac{1}{2}"$ each

2 plated steel slotted flat shelf supports,
   $3' \times 1\frac{3}{8}"$ each

3 pieces of pine, $6' \times 12" \times 2"$ each

2 pieces of pine, $6' \times 2" \times 1"$ each

32 flat washers, $\frac{1}{4}"$

32 zinc bolts and nuts, $\frac{1}{4}$-$20 \times \frac{1}{2}"$ round

32 lock washers, $\frac{1}{4}"$

1 quart polyurethane, optional

TOOLS

Builder's square

Phillips-head screwdriver

$\frac{7}{16}"$ wrench

Hacksaw or jigsaw with a metal-cutting
   blade

Drill with a 1" spade bit

$\frac{3}{4}"$ wood chisel

Hammer

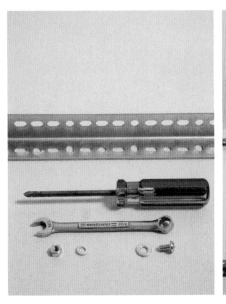
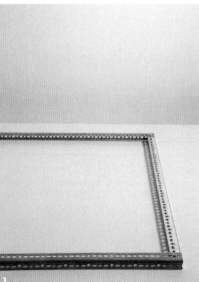
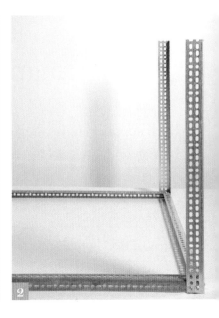

1. Place the two 6'-long shelf supports parallel to each other, flat sides up. Place two 3' × 1½" × 1½" shelf supports perpendicular to them, flat sides up, to make a rectangle. Align the short pieces so that their corners are flush with the edges of the long pieces. Thread a flat washer onto a bolt and slide it through the corner hole. Thread a lock washer onto the bolt on the underside and secure it with the nut, tightening it only with your fingers for now. Repeat on the three remaining corners. Use the screwdriver to tighten the bolts, but not all of the way. Align the builder's square with the corners of the frame to make sure they are square. Use the wrench on the underside and the screwdriver on the top to tighten the bolts for the final time. Flip the frame over and set it aside.

2. Use the hacksaw to cut each 3' × 2¼" × 1½" slotted steel piece to 29¾" long. Align one of these legs with the outside of a corner, with the long side of the leg running along the long side of the table. Fasten the leg to the table, using the nuts, washers, lock washers, and bolts as you did in Step 1. Use two on the widest side of the leg and one on the other. Repeat at all three corners.

3. Stand the table on its legs. Using the square as you did in Step 1, align it with each corner to make sure they are square. Tighten the bolts one final time with the wrench and the screwdriver.

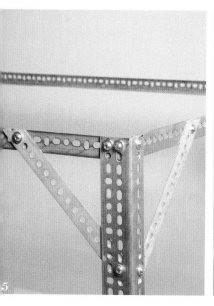

4. Position one 3' × 1⅜" shelf support on the diagonal from the leg to the top of the frame, 8" below the top of the frame and 8½" from the corner, lining up the holes in the frame with the holes in the shelf support. Mark your cutting lines with a pencil; the marks should be at an angle so that the ends of the cut braces are flush with the outside of the table legs and the top of the table. Mark the remaining shelf supports in the same way, so that you have eight braces total. Use the hacksaw to cut out the braces along the pencil marks.

5. Position a brace on a leg and the long side of the frame, with the brace running along the inside of the leg and the outside of the frame. Fasten as above, with a nut, washer, lock washer, and bolt. Repeat with a second brace for that leg, running it along the short side. Repeat in the remaining three corners.

6. Place all but the middle 6' × 12" × 2" board in the frame. Mark the boards where they touch the bolts on either end of the table. Remove the boards from the table and use the drill with the spade bit to drill into the sides of the boards at their centers, where the pencil marks are. Fit the boards back into the frame; if your holes don't line up nicely, use a wood chisel and hammer to expand the holes to fit.

7. Drop the middle board into the frame, then put one of the 6' × 2" × 1" lengths of pine on either side of it to fill in the gaps. If desired, apply a coat of polyurethane to the tabletop to seal it.

Parchment-Top Table

There are dozens of varieties of cement board available in a range of thicknesses. We used HardieBacker 500, an easy-to-find brand at the big-box hardware stores.

We happened to find this rimmed side table marooned on the sidewalk in our neighborhood. Because it has a rim, we needed do nothing more than prepare the cement board and drop it right into the top. For a rimless tabletop, you'll need to secure the cement board with a bit of adhesive.

MATERIALS

5' × 3' × ⅜" sheet cement board

1 pint clear shellac

TOOLS

Steel measuring tape

Carpenter's square

Handsaw

60-grit sandpaper

2" oil or all-paints paintbrush

Construction adhesive, such as Liquid Nails

1. For a rimmed tabletop, use a steel measuring tape to measure the length and width of the inset along the inside edge of the rim. If you're making the top for a rimless table, measure the length and width of the table along the edges. Use a measuring tape and a pencil to mark the dimensions of your table on the cement board. Use a carpenter's square to connect the marks to ensure that the lines are straight and the angles are square.

2. Use a handsaw to cut out the tabletop along the pencil lines. The edges of the board will be quite rough. Use 60-grit sandpaper to sand the edges, gently rounding the corners until they are smooth to the touch. Wipe down the board with a soft cloth. Apply a coat of shellac to the top and edges of the board and let it dry for at least one hour. Apply a second coat and let it dry for another hour.

3. If you're making a top for a rimless table, apply a thin coat of construction adhesive to the wrong side of the shellacked board. Flip the top over and set it onto the table, making sure that the edges of the board are flush with the edges of the table. For a rimmed table, simply set the "parchment" inside the rim.

Nuts and Bolts

Brush Care

Clean brushes used to apply shellac with denatured alcohol rather than mineral spirits, which won't do the job on alcohol-based mixtures.

Space-Age Coffee Table

To fasten the tiers together, you need to assemble the base without screwing anything together, and then disassemble it in vertical sections, which is not exactly an intuitive process, given the way the base is stacked.

MATERIALS

8 90-degree galvanized elbows, 7" each

4 90-degree galvanized elbows, 4" each

8 zinc bolts and nuts, 8=1" × 32

12 #6 sheet metal screws, ½" each

36" × 1" round solid pine panel

1 quart primer

½ quart paint in desired color (we used Benjamin Moore Soot/#2129-20)

Industrial strength adhesive-backed Velcro, 36" × 2" strip

TOOLS

Black permanent marker

Drill with ³⁄₁₆" and ⅛" bits

Phillips-head screwdriver

120-grit sandpaper

2" all-paints paintbrush

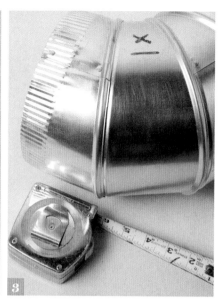

1. Join four 7" elbows to form a circle. Repeat with the remaining 7" elbows, and then join the 4" elbows to make a smaller circle.

2. Stack the circles on top of one another to form tiers, aligning the ribs and placing the smaller tier in the middle. Find the seams where two elbows meet. On the ribs adjacent to the seams, mark the tiers deep in the middle, where they meet, with a horizontal line.

3. Pull the stack apart in half vertically, making note of the top and bottom of the base. Using the marks as guides, mark an X 1" beyond them, toward the center. Use a drill with a $\frac{3}{16}$" bit to drill a hole at each X.

4. Break the tiers into quarters so you can fasten one quarter of the base together at a time. Rest the elbows on a work surface so that the openings of the elbows are facing you. Align the holes, slide the bolt through, and fasten the nut with your hands. Don't fasten it too tightly—once you put the entire base together, you'll need a little room to play. Repeat with the remaining three sections of the base.

5. Put two sections together to make half the base. Use an ⅛" bit to drill a hole ½" from the seam on each tier, through two layers of elbow. Screw in the sheet metal screws. Repeat on the other half of the base. Put the two halves together. Screw them together in the same manner, drilling a hole ½" from the seam on each tier, through two layers of elbow, and fasten with the sheet metal screws. Set the base aside.

6. Sand the top, bottom, and edge of the pine round. Wipe it down with a soft cloth, brush a thin coat of primer on the top and edge, and let it dry. Brush a thin coat of primer on the bottom and let it dry. Sand the round all over and wipe it down with a soft cloth again. Apply a coat of paint on the top and edge and let it dry. Apply a coat of paint on the bottom and let it dry.

7. Cut the Velcro into twelve 3" pieces. Separate the hooks from the loops. Wipe down the top of the table base with a soft cloth to remove any traces of grease or residue. Remove the adhesive backing from one of the loop pieces and fasten it 3½" from the outer edge of the base, along a rib. (This is the high point, where the tabletop makes contact with the base.) Repeat with the remaining loop pieces and ribs.

8. To determine where to put the hook sides of the Velcro on the underside of the table, set it on top of the base. Use a pencil to mark the underside of the tabletop where the Velcro is attached to the base. This is where the outside long edge of the hook sides of the Velcro should be attached. Place the tabletop wrong side up on a work surface. Remove the adhesive from the hook pieces of the Velcro and fasten them to the table, using your pencil marks as guides. Flip the tabletop over and set it onto the base, aligning the Velcro pieces.

Two-Hour Chair

The only time-consuming step in making this chair is cutting the shelf supports. Unlike the table, which is all right angles, this chair is designed to conform to the way we sit, which is always leaning back slightly. To achieve this, the chair base is smaller than the seat. If you want to make a perfectly square chair, make the sled legs 18 inches long.

MATERIALS

2 plated steel slotted angle shelf supports, 3' × 1½" × 1½" each

9 plated steel slotted angle shelf supports, 18" × 1½" × 1½" each

2 plated steel slotted angle shelf supports, 15" × 1½" × 1½" each

18 zinc bolts and nuts, ½-20 × ½" each

18 flat washers, ½" each

18 lock washers, ½" each

18"-square piece of ¾" plywood

TOOLS

Phillips-head screwdriver

7⁄16" wrench

1. Arrange the 3' lengths on a work surface, flat edge down, so that they are parallel. Position an 18" piece on either end so that the edges are flush, and place another 18" piece 15½" from one short edge. Fasten them together by sliding a flat washer onto the bolt and inserting it into a corner hole from the underside of the frame. Slide a lock washer onto the bolt, followed by the nut, and tighten with the wrench. This is the back of the chair.

2. Position an 18" shelf support on each end of the ledge of the support in the middle of the chair back. Fasten them to the frame along the inside edge and middle support, using the washers, nuts, and bolts as you did in Step 1. Fasten a third 18" shelf support across the front of the seat in the same manner.

3. Attach the 15" shelf supports to the outside of the bottom of the frame. Fasten an 18" piece across the front of the base.

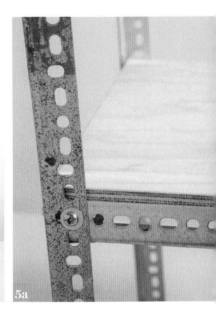

4. With the chair front facing you, tilt the frame by pulling the seat toward you and pushing the chair back away from you. Attach the front legs as in step 3, mounting the remaining two 18" shelf supports to the outside of the seat and base frame. Once it's completely assembled, work around the chair to tighten each bolt.

5. Set the plywood into the seat frame so that it rests on the bolts; it will be slightly higher than the edges of the frame (see 5a), so that your legs are not touching the frame when you're seated. If the plywood resists, use a hammer to tap it into place.

2

Lighting

Rope-Wrapped Lamp

This thin rope is a bricklayer's best friend—it's an essential guide for laying bricks straight. A standard package comes in 200-foot skeins, and once you start using this rope, you'll want to wrap it around every piece of furniture in the house. (See page 152 for another mason line–inspired project.)

MATERIALS

Empty tuna can, 12 ounces or larger

Wooden lamp base, 18" tall

1 quart primer

200' natural cotton mason line

TOOLS

Wire snips

120-grit sandpaper

1" all-paints paintbrush

Cloth tape measure

Very sharp scissors

1 9-ounce package (2 bottles)
    two-part epoxy

1. Use wire snips to cut a V-shaped notch out of the tuna can. (The can serves as a working base; you'll set the lamp on top with the cord tucked inside.)

2. Sand the lamp base all over, then use a soft cloth to remove any dust. Apply a thin coat of primer and let it dry. To work around the lamp cord on the base of the lamp, you'll need to cut pieces of rope to accommodate it before you begin wrapping the rest of the lamp. Use a cloth tape measure to measure the circumference of the base, beginning and ending at the lamp cord. Using very sharp scissors, cut pieces of mason line that length to wrap the base up to the top edge of the cord. Discard any pieces of mason line with frayed ends. Set the lamp base on top of the tuna can with the cord nestled inside and the cord entry point sitting in the V.

3. Prepare a half-dollar–size mixture of the epoxy and, using a trimmed paint stirrer (see page 101), apply a thin coat of it around the base, stopping even with the top of the cord. Working from the bottom left of the cord, wrap the lengths of mason line around the lamp until they're even with the top edge of the cord. Once you've worked around the cord, begin wrapping and gluing a continuous piece of mason line around the remainder of the lamp, applying the epoxy to about 1½" of the lamp at a time. Mix up additional half-dollar–size batches of the epoxy as needed. Before you cut the mason line, let the epoxy dry thoroughly. Use very sharp scissors for the final cut.

Ode to Giacometti Wall Sconce

If you have a porcelain socket mounted to the wall, you can clip this right onto it to make a wall sconce. To make a pendant lamp, bend the tabs on the ductwork over into tight U shapes, attach a chain to the tabs, and hang it from a ceiling canopy.

MATERIALS

8" vent cap

4 washers, 1¼" each

Bulb adapter

1 can (13 ounces) spray primer

TOOLS

Tin snips

120-grit sandpaper

Two-part epoxy

1. Use tin snips to cut the collar off of the vent cap at the top edge, leaving the three tabs intact. Fold the tabs back onto themselves.

   Thread all four washers onto the clip-on bulb adapter and use the nut to secure them as tightly as possible. Use 120-grit sandpaper to rough up the inside center of the cap. Prepare a quarter-size pool of two-part epoxy and spread it on the center of the cap. Prop up the cap so that it's level. Place the adapter in the epoxy and let it set.

2. Spray the exterior of the cap all over with primer. Let it dry. Snap the sconce onto the lightbulb.

Molecular Desk Light

If you can screw in a lightbulb, you can make this versatile light. Thread it into a ceiling socket and grow it as you please, or stick to the restrained version we put together, which is nicely scaled for a desktop. Your options are only limited by the number of adapters the hardware store has in stock.

MATERIALS

Medium twin light or single-to-double adapters

Turn knob socket kit

7-watt appliance bulbs

TOOLS

Your hands

1. Screw one adapter into another and just keep going, using as many adapters as you like. We left one socket in each adapter open for a bulb, filling the other with another adapter.

2. Assemble the turn knob socket kit according to the package instructions. Screw one adapter into it. Screw a lightbulb into each open socket, plug the light in, and turn it on.

Constructivist Lamp

When you're cutting with the jigsaw, hold it still and turn the grate around the blade, rather than moving the jigsaw itself.

MATERIALS

6" atrium grate

2 atrium grates, 4" each

3" atrium grate

Strainer dome cover

1 can (13 ounces) spray primer

1 can (12 ounces) ultraflat black interior-exterior spray paint

2 round head stove bolts with nuts, 8-32 × ½" each

2 #8 washers

3-way socket kit

TOOLS

Jigsaw

Drill with ³⁄₁₆" and ³⁄₈" bits

120-grit sandpaper

Phillips-head screwdriver

Two-part epoxy

Pliers

1. Use a jigsaw to cut away the collar on each atrium grate: On the largest grate, cut up to the tabs; on the others, cut the two bottommost sections only. Use a drill with a $\frac{3}{16}$" bit to drill a hole in the bottom center of each grate. Use a $\frac{3}{8}$" bit to drill through the center hole of the strainer dome cover. Sand the top of the dome and the interiors and exteriors of the grates with the sandpaper.

2. Spray the top of the dome and the insides of the grates with primer and let them dry. Spray the outsides of each with primer and let them dry. Repeat with the flat black paint, spraying the interiors of the grates first, followed by the exteriors.

3. Place the 6" grate right side up on a clean work surface. Set the top of a 4" grate on top of it, aligning the holes. Fasten the two together, pushing the bolt through the hole in the small grate and then through the larger one. Thread a washer onto the bolt end and then screw on the nut, using a Phillips-head screwdriver to fasten it tightly. Set aside. Place the second 4" grate right side up on the work surface. Set the top of the 3" grate on top of it, aligning the holes. Fasten the two together, pushing the bolt through the hole in the small grate and then through the larger one. Thread a washer onto the bolt end and then screw on the nut, using a Phillips-head screwdriver to fasten it tightly. Set the bottom of the base (the 6" and 4" pieces) on the work surface. Prepare a quarter-size mixture of the epoxy. Use a trimmed paint stirrer (see page 101) to apply a thin coat of the epoxy along the rim of the 4" grate. Set the other 4" grate on top of it, aligning the edges. Let the epoxy dry.

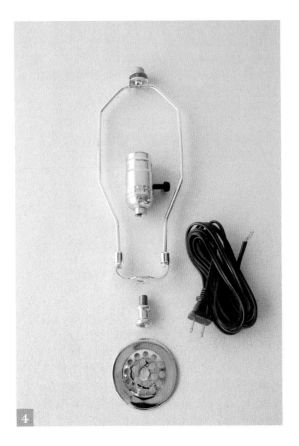

4. Assemble the socket kit, inserting the nipple of the socket into the center hole of the strainer dome cover (which essentially acts like a giant washer). Fasten it with the nut enclosed in the socket kit, using pliers to tighten it. Set aside. Thread the electric cord, exposed wires leading, up through the lamp base. Begin at the vertical openings of the base, snaking it up through the center openings of the other grates, and finally through the socket nipple. Connect the wires to the two terminals on the socket switch according to the package directions. Attach the switch to the base.

5. Prepare a dime-size mixture of epoxy. Use a trimmed paint stirrer to apply a thin bead of epoxy around the rim of the top grate. Set the strainer dome cover and socket on it, aligning the edges. Let the epoxy dry. Touch up the base with the flat black paint, if necessary.

Five-Minute Desk Lamp

No tools, no glue, no nuts, bolts, or screws. Just slide the clamp onto the wood base and clip the light on top.

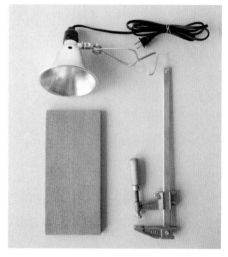

MATERIALS

Clamp light with reflector

12" × 6" × 1" piece of cedar

16" bar clamp

TOOLS

Your hands

If desired, trim the grips off of the clamp light with a utility knife. Slide the clamp onto the middle of the piece of cedar. Clip the clamp light onto the end of the bar clamp. That's it.

Mrs. Astor's Chandelier

You'll need a large work surface and a place to hang the chandelier while you're working on it. A doorjamb fitted with a cup hook is ideal. A pair of top-quality needle-nose pliers with a sharp cutting blade is essential. The lower the wire number, the thicker it is; the thicker the gauge of the wire you use, the better the chandelier will hold its shape. Working with thicker wire, however, requires strong hands.

The measurements and quantities listed below are for the chandelier pictured, but you can improvise or design your own using the same techniques we used here. To appreciate this chandelier, you have to embrace its imperfect balance—otherwise you'll go crazy trying to get it to hang perfectly straight.

NUTS AND BOLTS

Toggle Bolt Tutorial

Toggle bolts are used for hanging heavy items, typically from the ceiling, if the ceiling is constructed of drywall (There's no beam or stud in which to insert a screw eye or bolt). A toggle bolt has collapsible arms that, when pushed through a predrilled hole, open and straddle the hole. Bolts are typically screwed into them, but we substituted a large screw eye for hanging Mrs. Astor's Chandelier, because it's not as heavy as a traditional chandelier. To hang it, install the toggle bolt, screw the screw eye into it, and hang from the key ring.

How to Install a Toggle Bolt

To install a toggle bolt, first determine the size you need based on the weight of the object you want to hang. The heavier the object, the longer and wider the toggle bolt must be. Predrill a hole using a drill bit that is as wide as the toggle. Thread the bolt (or screw eye, as the case may be) into the underside of the toggle, then tap the toggle, wing-ends first, through the predrilled hole. Use a screwdriver to tighten the bolt or an awl to tighten a screw eye. Be aware that when used on a wall, the toggle will drop if the bolt or screw eye is removed.

MATERIALS

½ yard kraft paper

10-gauge galvanized wire, 12'

22-gauge galvanized wire, 4'

#16 single jack zinc-plated chain, 20'

6 key rings, 1½" diameter each

13 key rings, 1" diameter each

4 key rings, ¾" diameter each

4 emergency candles, 4" long each

White or gray poster board or gift
    box–grade cardboard

¼" flat washer

⅛" screw eye

⅛" toggle bolt

TOOLS

Permanent marker

Tongue-and-groove, or locking, pliers

8" needle-nose pliers

Drill with a 5⁄64" bit

Utility knife

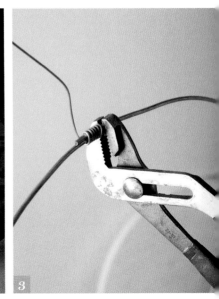

1. Measure and mark a circle with a diameter of 24³⁄₈" on the kraft paper. Measure and mark a circle with a 17" diameter inside the larger circle. Divide the circles into eight equal wedges—each mark should be a little more than 3" apart around the circumference of the larger circle and 2¹⁄₈" apart around the circumference of the smaller circle.

2. Run a length of 10-gauge wire around the circumference of each drawn circle, adding 3" for overlap. Mark the wire with a permanent marker where the circles and the wedges intersect.

3. Use 1' of the 22-gauge wire to wire together the cut ends of the larger tier where they overlap. When you've wound the fastening wire around the tier twice, place the tongue-and-groove pliers on the tier and the wound wire, to lock the end in place. Continue winding the wire around the tier to fasten it securely. Repeat with the smaller tier.

4. Working with the large tier first, use the needle-nose pliers and tongue-and-groove pliers to make a crimp at each marked spot, alternating between 1½"-deep crimps and 1"-deep crimps as you work your way around the tier. On the smaller tier, make 1"-deep crimps, alternating the peaks to point inside and outside the tier. Set both tiers aside.

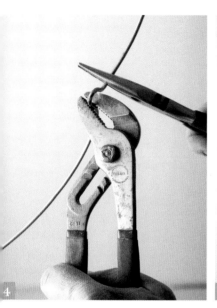
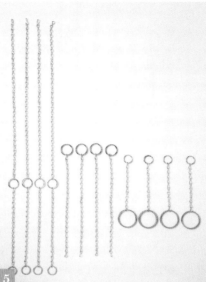

5. Use the needle-nose pliers to unlink the pieces of chain to make the chain drops. For the topmost drop, undo four 12" pieces of chain and four 6" pieces of chain. For the bottom drop, undo four 4½" pieces of chain and four 8" pieces of chain.

To assemble the uppermost chain, connect a 12" piece of chain to a 6" piece of chain with a 1" key ring. Slip a second 1" key ring onto the other end of the 6" chain. Repeat three more times to make a total of four drops.

To assemble the bottom drops, attach a 1½" key ring to each of the four 4½"-long chains. On the opposite ends, attach a ¾" key ring. Attach a 1" key ring to one end of each of the remaining four 8" pieces of chain.

6. To assemble the chandelier, attach the loose ends of the uppermost chains to a 1" key ring. (It's easiest to put the chandelier together from this stage by hanging it from a cup hook screwed into a doorjamb.) Working on one large crimp at a time, slip the large key ring attached to a 4½" bottom drop chain over the crimp from the outside of the tier, then attach the key ring of the upper chain to the crimp. Repeat this with the remaining three upper chains.

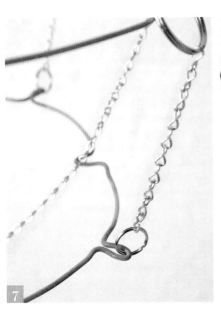  

7. Attach the bottom tier by first attaching the small key rings on the 4½" chains to the crimps running outside the perimeter of the tier.

8. Next, slide the key-ring ends of the 8"-long drops onto the small crimps of the large tier, working from the inside of the tier. Guide them through the crimps on the bottom tier that point toward the interior of the tier.

9. Thread the loose ends of the chains onto a 1½" key ring. For the bottom flourish, use the needle-nose pliers to unlink the pieces of chain to make four 4" lengths of chain. Thread these onto the same 1½" key ring and slide the loose ends onto the last remaining 1½" key ring.

10. To make the arms, cut four 12" pieces of 22-gauge wire. Thread one wire through a small crimp on the top tier. Secure the end around one side of the crimp. Wrap the wire around the crimp three times, ending on the

back side and threading the wire through the crimp to the front. Make a loop, with the end of the wire pointing upward. Repeat with the remaining three pieces of wire.

11. Using a $\frac{5}{64}$" bit, drill 1½" into the center of the bottom of each candle. To make the bobeches, use a 2"- to 2½"-wide jar lid as a template. Trace four circles onto the poster board. To find the center of the bobeche, draw vertical and horizontal lines through the center of each circle. Set the candle on the bobeche where the lines meet, and trace around the candle. Cut out the bobeches and use a utility knife to cut out the candle hole, cutting about ⅛" inside the pencil mark. Score around the hole, stopping at the pencil mark, to create a fringed rim. Repeat with the remaining three bobeches. Slide each candle through a bobeche, then place one on each arm.

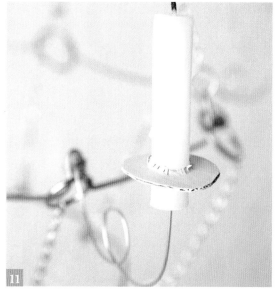

12. To hang the chandelier, thread the washer onto the screw eye, then screw the screw eye into the toggle bolt. Install the toggle bolt (see page 94) and screw eye. Thread the key ring at the top of the chandelier onto the screw eye, and make adjustments to the chain as necessary. Light the candles and break out the champagne.

NUTS AND BOLTS

How to Determine the Circumference of the Tiers

If you want to make larger or smaller tiers, simply plug in the desired diameter and leave the rest of the formulas below unchanged.

For the larger tier, our finished diameter is 18", so:

3.14 (pi) × 18" (diameter) + 20 [(4 large crimps × 3" each) + (4 small crimps × 2" each)] = approximately $76\frac{1}{2}$" circumference.

To find the diameter of the uncrimped circle:

$76\frac{1}{2}$" (circumference) ÷ 3.14 (pi) = approximately $24\frac{3}{8}$"

For the smaller tier, our finished diameter is 12", so:

3.14 (pi) × 12" (diameter) + 16 (8 small crimps × 2" each) = approximately $53\frac{3}{4}$" circumference.

To find the diameter of the uncrimped circle:

$53\frac{3}{4}$" (circumference) ÷ 3.14 (pi) = approximately 17"

Honeycomb Lamp Shade

Quick-dry craft glue dries clear, which is essential for a professional look. It's available at most craft stores. If you're more comfortable cutting the shade cover slightly larger than the dimensions of the shade, do so, and then trim the excess.

MATERIALS

4' × 2' rug pad

15" drum shade

TOOLS

Yardstick

Square

Sharp scissors

Wooden clothespins

Quick-dry craft glue

Painter's tape

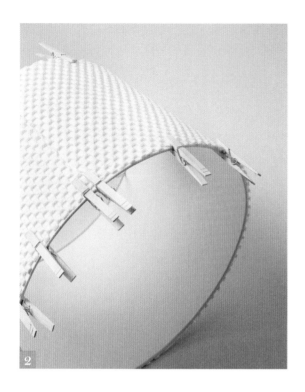

1. To determine the circumference of the shade cover, multiply the diameter of the shade by 3.14. In this case, 15" × 3.14 = approximately 47⅛". Use a yardstick to mark the rug pad with a straight 47⅛"-long line close to one long edge.

Measure the height of your shade. (Ours was 8".) Place the outer edge of the square at the end of the line and mark the pad with the appropriate height measurement from your first line. Do this at several points along the length of the first line. Using the yardstick, connect the marks to make a 47⅛" line that is parallel to the one below it. Use the square to close both ends of the parallel lines to make a rectangle. Cut out the rectangle with sharp scissors.

2. Wrap the pad around the shade, beginning and ending at the back seam of the shade. Use clothespins to hold the pad in place. Run a thick bead of quick-dry craft glue along the back seam where the edges of the pad meet. Attach the pad, pressing down gently with the palm of your hand. Affix a length of painter's tape along the seam to hold the pad in place. Let the glue dry thoroughly before you remove the tape and clothespins.

Periscope Lamp

The trick to putting together these relatively simple-to-make lights is to assemble the correct materials. The elbow must be crimped, because the crimps provide the inside ledge on which you rest the Plexiglas. Be sure that the epoxy you purchase will stick to plastic—there are several different versions, so read the packages carefully before you buy. The electrical cord comes in a kit with everything you need to wire the lamp: socket, plug, and switch, plus instructions on how to put it all together.

MATERIALS

8" fiberboard-backed cork mat

1 quart primer

Sample pot neutral paint such as stone or slate, in eggshell finish

24-gauge 6" crimp elbow

Black foam insulation with adhesive back, 9" × ¾" strip

5⅞" × ⅛" round piece of frosted Plexiglas

Electrical cord with socket, plug, and switch

660-watt/250-volt porcelain lamp holder

2 #6 wood screws, ¾" each

40-watt lightbulbs

TOOLS

2" all-paints paintbrush

Tin snips

Two-part, five-minute epoxy that works on plastic and dries clear

Awl

Phillips-head screwdriver

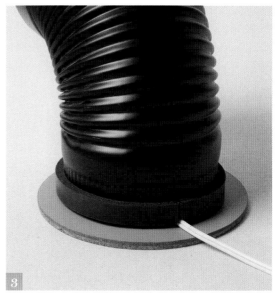

1. Prime and paint the fiberboard side of the cork mat. Set aside to dry. On the ridged end of the elbow, at the center of the back, use the tin snips to snip a V-shaped notch $\frac{1}{2}$" deep. (This is where the electrical cord will come out of the light.) Remove the protective backing from the foam insulation and wrap it around the bottom of the elbow, aligning the edge of the foam with the edge of the elbow.

2. On a piece of scrap cardboard, mix a dime-size pool of epoxy. Apply a tiny dollop of epoxy to the ledge inside the elbow at four points equidistant from each other. Slide your hand in through the other end of the elbow, drop the Plexiglas into the end with the ledge, and use your hand to guide it into place. Set the elbow on its curve and prop it up to keep the Plexiglas in place. Let the epoxy dry according to the package instructions.

3. Wire the electrical socket into the lamp holder according to the package instructions. Center the lamp holder on the painted side of the cork mat and screw it into place using the wood screws. Screw in a lightbulb—we used 40-watt bulbs to provide a nice glow—and set the elbow over it, positioning it so that the notch and the electrical cord are aligned.

Instant Candelabrum

You can make the arms on the candelabrum longer (it's easy to get carried away!), but at a certain length, you'll need to add larger bushings to the base to support them.

Plumbing Ts are also known as straight tees and reducing tees; hex bushings are used to join pipes of dissimilar sizes. The size of each fitting is stamped on its side, but it's not always legible, so verify sizes by loosely putting the parts together at the store before buying them.

If the parts are difficult to screw together, put a little 3-in-one oil on the threads to lubricate them—and put on a pair of work gloves to protect your hands.

MATERIALS

2" × 1¼" hex bushing

1¼" × 1" hex bushing

1" × ¾" hex bushing

¾" × ½" hex bushing

5 nipples, 1" each

5 plumbing Ts, ½" each

4 candles, 1" diameter

TOOLS

Your hands

1. Use a soft cloth to wipe away the oil coating on each plumbing part. Screw the 1¼" bushing into the 2" bushing, making three full turns to secure it. Proceed with the 1" and ¾" bushings in a similar manner, ending with the smallest bushing. Set aside.

2. To make the arms, screw a nipple into either side of one of the Ts. This will be the center of the candelabrum. Screw a T into each nipple, turning it a few times and ending with the center hole facing the opposite direction of the one in the center. Repeat with the remaining nipples and Ts, fastening two on either side of the center. Screw a nipple into the open hole on the center piece. Join the arm to the base by screwing the nipple into the top of the base, turning it until it is secure.

NUTS AND BOLTS

Playing with Plumbing Parts

Metal plumbing parts are typically coated with oil to prevent them from rusting. Before screwing them together, wipe them down with a soft cloth to remove the excess oil. If these pieces are exposed to prolonged periods of damp air (if they're left out on the patio, for example), they will eventually rust. Rub them down with 3-in-one oil (the same stuff you use to grease a bike chain) to prevent this.

Machine-Age Candlesticks

If you can screw in a lightbulb, you can make these candlesticks. To prepare the bushings, see page 105. The instructions below are for making one candlestick, but the more of these you have clustered together on your dining room table or mantel, the better.

MATERIALS

$1\frac{1}{2}$" × $1\frac{1}{4}$" hex bushing

$1\frac{1}{4}$" × 1" hex bushing

1" × $\frac{3}{4}$" hex bushing

$\frac{3}{4}$" × $\frac{1}{2}$" hex bushing

$1\frac{1}{2}$" union

Taper candle

TOOLS

Your hands

1. Wipe down each plumbing part with a soft cloth (see Playing with Plumbing Parts on page 105). Screw the threaded end of the $1\frac{1}{2}$" bushing into one end of the union. Continue screwing the bushings into one another, working from largest to smallest.

2. Trim around the bottom $\frac{1}{4}$" of a standard taper candle to make it fit into the bushing opening.

3

Walls

Sterling Striped Wallpaper

Before you begin, bring a roll of the tape to the paint store and buy a sample pot of the color you are considering for your walls. Test the combination of the tape and the paint color on a board before committing a whole room or even a single wall to it.

MATERIALS

2½" HVAC foil tape

TOOLS

Metal yardstick
4' level
Steel measuring tape
Utility knife

1. Determine the amount of foil tape you will need (see Nuts and Bolts on the opposite page). Use the metal yardstick to mark 5" intervals along the bottom of the wall.

Align a level with the marks and lightly mark the wall at intervals all the way up to the ceiling, moving the level as you go. Use the level to connect the marks, making vertical lines 5" apart from one another.

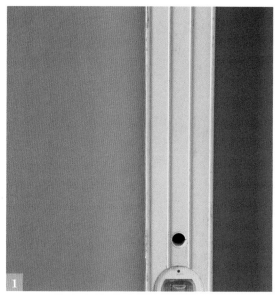

2. Use a tape measure to measure the length of each line, and record the measurements on a piece of paper. (If you live in an old house, there's a good chance the height of the wall will vary.) Add 2" to each measurement and cut pieces of tape to the recorded lengths.

3. Remove the protective backing from your first strip and, leaving an excess inch at the ceiling, work from the ceiling down to the floor. Affix the tape to the wall, rubbing it to remove any creases as you go. Continue affixing the strips to the wall on the marked lines. Once you've applied all of the strips, use a utility knife to cut away the excess at the top and bottom of each strip.

Nuts and Bolts

How Much Tape Do You Need?

Because the tape is $2\frac{1}{2}$ inches wide and the intervals between the strips are $2\frac{1}{2}$ inches wide, you are essentially covering half the wall in foil tape. To determine how much you need, convert the length of the wall into inches and divide it by 5. Multiply that number by the height of the wall, and then add 3 feet for wiggle room. For example, the wall we covered is 18 feet long × 8 feet tall. We used: [(18 feet × 12 inches) ÷ 5] × 8 feet + 3 feet = about 349 linear feet.

Soft-Touch Switch Plate

Be sure your utility knife is extrasharp; you want the edges of the switch plate to be crisp.

MATERIALS

12"-square cork tile, $^{3}/_{16}$" thick

TOOLS

Sharp utility knife

Ruler or metal tape measure

Wood glue

100-grit sandpaper

Brown permanent marker

1. Place the cork tile on a clean work surface. Remove the old switch plate from the wall and set aside the screws. Place the switch plate, right side up, on the cork tile, and use a pencil to trace around the perimeter and in the switch and screw holes. Cut out the switch plate and holes with a utility knife. Put the old switch plate back on the cork tile and trace only around the perimeter. Using a pencil and ruler, mark ¼" in from the edge of this rectangle. Use the utility knife to cut out the cork frame.

2. Place the cork switch plate wrong side up on the work surface. Apply a thin bead of wood glue around the rim of the cork frame. Line it up on the switch plate so that all of the edges are flush, and press firmly around the rim. Wipe away any excess glue. Weight it down with a heavy book and let it dry overnight. Sand the edges with the sandpaper to gently round them.

3. Attach the switch plate to the wall with the existing screws. If the screw heads clash with the color of the cork, color them with a brown permanent marker.

Lacy Room Divider

Quikrete WalkMakers (www.walkmaker.com) are used to lay patio walkways. The walls of the mold are on an angle, making it essential that you drill the holes for fastening nuts and bolts exactly as instructed below.

We hung this "wall" from an exposed pipe, but you can hang it from a beam, exposed or not. The finished piece is rather heavy and shouldn't be hung where there's no beam or joist to suspend it from. However you decide to hang it, enlist the help of one or two strong friends to give you a hand.

MATERIALS

16 stone molds

48 stove bolts and nuts, 8-32 × $\frac{3}{4}$"

4 screw eye bolts and nuts, 2" × $\frac{1}{2}$" each

10' cable, $\frac{1}{16}$" diameter

8 crimps, $\frac{1}{16}$" each

4 open screw eyes, 2" × $\frac{1}{2}$" each (if hanging from a beam)

TOOLS

Jigsaw or handsaw

Drill with an $\frac{8}{32}$" bit

Vise grips

1. Use a jigsaw or handsaw to trim the tiny tabs off each mold. Lay out the molds on the floor in your desired pattern.

2. Each side of each mold has either a center peak or a center valley. Holding two adjacent molds tightly together, drill a hole in one mold on either side of the peak or valley, equidistant from the adjacent peak or valley, drilling all the way through the first mold and allowing the drill bit to nick the second.

3. Pull the first mold away and drill a hole through the second, using the nick as your guide. Repeat with the remaining molds, drilling holes in the same manner.

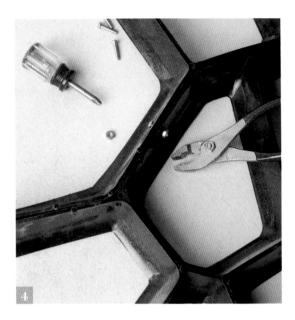

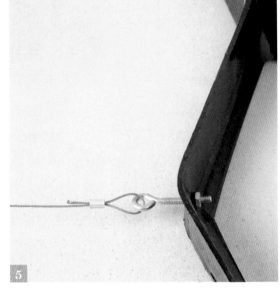

4. Use the nuts and stove bolts to fasten the panels together at the holes.

5. Drill holes in the top of the panel at each peak. Screw the screw eyes into the holes, about $\frac{1}{2}$" through to the other side, and thread on the nuts. Determine how close to the ceiling you want the panel to be. Double that number and add 6" or so. (We hung ours 1' from the pipe, so we cut 32" pieces of cable: 12" × 2 + 8" = 32".)

Thread a piece of cable through a crimp, then through the screw eye, and then pull 4" of the cable back through the crimp. The crimp should be positioned 1" from the screw eye. Use the vise grip to crush the crimp closed. Repeat with the remaining cables and crimps.

6. To suspend the room divider from an exposed pipe, thread the loose end of the cable through a crimp, around the pipe, and back through the crimp, as in Step 5. Crush the crimp closed with the vice grip.

7. To hang from a beam, first measure the distance between the screw eyes on the panel. Measure and mark the beam at these distances. Use the $\frac{8}{32}$" bit to drill pilot holes into the beam at each mark. Screw the open screw eyes into the holes, using an awl to tighten them. Thread the loose end of one cable through a crimp, through the screw eye, and then thread 4" of it back through the crimp. Position the crimp 3" from the top of the loop and use the vise grip to crush it. Repeat with the remaining cables.

Faux Boiserie

A perfectly mitered corner takes practice; pay attention to the way the angle on the molding has to slant *before* sawing it in the miter box. Chair rail comes in 8- to 10-foot lengths; if your walls are longer than that, you'll need to miter two lengths of molding together.

MATERIALS

Chair rail

$1\frac{1}{2}$" panel nails

1" panel nails

Screen molding

Wood Patch

Primer

Wall paint in desired color (we used Benjamin Moore Irongate/#1545 in eggshell)

TOOLS

Steel measuring tape

Level

Miter box

Countersink

Hammer

120-grit sandpaper

2" all-paints paintbrush

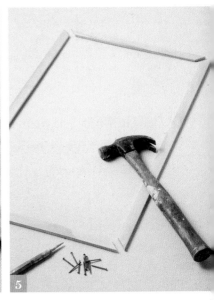

1. To determine how much chair rail you need, measure the perimeter of the room and add 10 percent to that. The standard height for chair rail is 36" from the floor to the top of the rail, but you can decide for yourself what height works best in your room. Use a measuring tape to make one pencil mark on the wall at this height. Using the level, work your way around the room, marking the wall at your chosen height.

2. You'll need to miter both ends of the chair rail to fit the length of the wall. Measure and mark the rail at a 45-degree angle. Set the chair rail in the miter box and choose the 45-degree angle guide for the cut. Insert the backsaw in the groove and cut the chair rail.

3. Nail the chair rail to the wall using the 1½" panel nails, aligning the top of the rail with the marks on the wall. Countersink (bury) each nail head by positioning the countersink on the head and banging it with a hammer.

4. Determine what size to make the paneled squares by first designing them on graph paper. The spaces in between each panel should be the same, as should the width and height of each panel. When you're happy with your design, use the measuring tape and level to transfer it onto the wall. (We positioned our panels 6" above the chair rail and 4" apart.)

5. Measure the length and width of each panel square you drew on the wall. Use the miter box to cut the screen molding accordingly.

6. Nail the screen molding to the wall using the 1" panel nails. Countersink the nail heads as you did in Step 3.

7. Use the Wood Patch to fill any gaps in the miters and cover the exposed nail heads. Let it dry according to the package instructions. Sand the patched area with the sandpaper. Prime and paint the wall your desired color.

"Wall" of Frames

Drop cloths are available in various sizes and weights and can be cut to size or stitched together depending on their use. If putting brush to canvas is not your strength, enlist an artist friend to paint the desired pattern on the drop cloth.

If you can't find hospital tracking locally, order it from Zarin Fabrics (www. zarinfabrics.com or 212-925-6112). We used their track system #9046.

MATERIALS

Drop cloths, washed and dried

Black acrylic artist paint

Heavy-duty drapery pins

$^{11}/_{16}$" wide × $^{1}/_{2}$" high ceiling curtain track system

Molded slides

2 track stops

Toggle bolts, if using

TOOLS

Drill

1" artist's brush

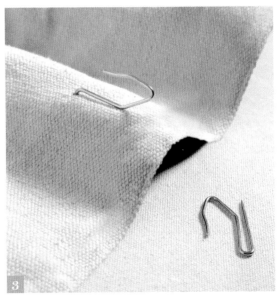

1. Measure the width of the space you want to cover. This is how much track hardware you will need. Multiply that width by 1.5. This is the amount of drop cloth you will need. (This allows for fabric fullness.) Determine the length of the canvas you need by measuring from floor to ceiling. Subtract $\frac{1}{2}$" to allow for the curtain hardware. If you need less drop cloth than the prepackaged variety is available in, mark and measure it and cut it to size. We marked and measured two drop cloths at $9\frac{1}{2}$', cut them to size, and, rather than stitching them together and creating a seam, hung them in two panels.

2. Paint the desired pattern on the drop cloth and let it dry thoroughly.

3. Fasten the drapery pins to the tops of the drop cloths, positioning them so that the top curve of the pin is flush with the top edge of the drop cloth. Fasten a pin every $\frac{1}{2}$" along the top of the curtain. Set aside.

4. Install the track by mounting the hardware to your ceiling through the holes in the track. If you're mounting on a part of the ceiling with no joist, install toggle bolts to add strength (see page 94). Attach one of the stops to the track and then slide on all of the slides. Attach the other stop at the opposite end. Working from one end of the "wall," slide a drapery pin into the tiny hole in each slide.

4

Decor

Folk Art Family Silhouettes

The head sizes of the cut tacks can be very inconsistent; use one of the smaller ones to make the point of the V in the eye. Refrain from driving any of the tacks all the way into the wood; this will give the piece dimension and let the light pick up shadows on the tacks. The materials listed below are for making five silhouettes.

MATERIALS

5 pieces $^3/_4$" birch plywood, 17" × 14" each

1 pint ebony stain

#3 × $^3/_8$" aluminum cut tacks

75 coated sinker nails, #4d 1$^3/_8$"

20' feet manila rope, $^1/_2$" thick

10 screw eyes, $^{13}/_{16}$"

Picture wire, 5'

TOOLS

120-grit sandpaper

Cotton cloth

Latex gloves

Steel ruler

Painter's tape

Hammer

Awl

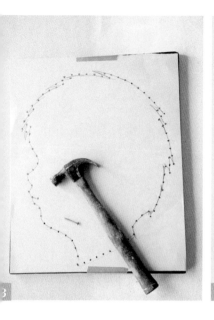

1. Sand the edges of the plywood boards with the sandpaper. Using a cotton cloth and wearing latex gloves, rub the stain into one side of each piece, going with the grain. Let the stain dry overnight.

2. Meanwhile, draw the silhouettes (see page 133). Mark the silhouette at the tip of the nose and lips and at the center of the eyeball. Working from these points and using a steel ruler, mark the silhouette at $\frac{1}{2}$" intervals. There's a fudge factor here—you can cheat the distance a little, where necessary; you just want enough space between the tacks so that the silhouette reads nicely. Repeat with the remaining silhouettes.

3. Center a silhouette on the stained side of one board and fasten with painter's tape. Use a coated sinker nail and a hammer to make pilot holes at each pencil mark.

4. Remove the piece of paper and drive the tacks into the pilot holes, beginning with the nose, lips, and eyeball and working your way around the silhouette.

5. Cut a 64" piece of manila rope on the diagonal. Beginning at the middle of the bottom edge, run the rope around the rim, nailing it to the plywood with the coated sinker nails every 4" to $4\frac{1}{2}$".

6. To make smooth corners, drive a nail into the frame on either side of the corner. Cut the rope end on the diagonal so that it fits smoothly against the other end of the rope.

7. Attach the screw eyes. Measure and mark the back of the portrait 5" from the top and $1\frac{1}{2}$" from the edge on both sides. Make a pilot hole with the awl. Screw the screw eye in as far as you can with your hand. Insert the awl into the screw eye and spin it around until it is flush with the wood. Fasten 12" of the picture wire to the screw eyes, sliding each end through a hole and twisting the wire back onto itself.

Chain-Link Mirror Frame

The white pads that punctuate the graphic pattern are designed to adhere to the bottoms of vases and trivets to protect surfaces from scratches.

MATERIALS

Primer, if painting the mirror frame

1 sample pot (see page 130) or ½ quart desired paint color in eggshell finish, if painting the mirror frame

1 flat-faced mirror frame

35 white and black die-cut vinyl zeroes, 3" each

35 heavy-duty white felt pads, ⅜" each

TOOLS

1" all-paints paintbrush

120-grit sandpaper, if painting the frame

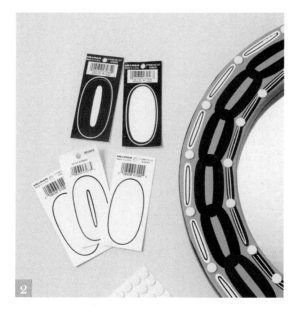

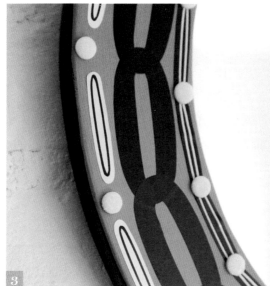

1. If it's not already painted a color you like, prime and paint the frame (see page 131).

2. Arrange the black vinyl zeroes around the center of the frame, overlapping them as you go. Once you've achieved the desired design, remove the backings from the numbers and affix them to the front face of the frame, slightly overlapping the numbers to give the illusion of a chain. Do not rub down.

3. Peel the interior of the black numbers off of their protective backings and affix them along the interior edge of the mirror, overlapping them as you go. Along the outside edge of the frame, affix the interiors of the white zeroes, leaving a $\frac{1}{2}$" space between each one. Affix the felt pads along the interior chain where the numbers meet. Affix them along the outside edge in the spaces between the numbers.

Faux 40s Mod Vase

Don't skimp on the PVC cement—it's what's sealing the bottom of the vase. If you use too little, the vase won't hold water.

MATERIALS

3" × 3" × 2½" × 1½" PVC double reducing wye

PVC cement

3" PVC flush cleanout

TOOLS

Your hands

On a clean work surface, set the wye wrong side up, with the arms facing downward. Slide your fingers into the indentation in the cleanout to hold it and apply a liberal about of PVC cement around the rim. Turn the wye right side up with your other hand and slide the cleanout into it until it meets the ridge. Set the wye wrong side up on the work surface and let it dry thoroughly, for about 2 hours, before filling it with water.

Clever Cuff Links

We didn't follow Jasper Johns's advice on this one (see page xi). We've done nothing to these screw posts other than strip them of their intended use. You'll need some help screwing them tight once they're in your shirt cuffs.

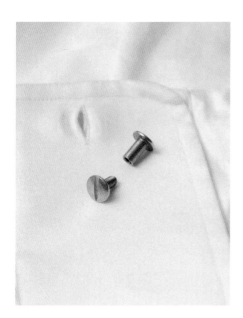

MATERIALS

2 brass screw posts, $\frac{1}{2}$" diameter each

TOOLS

A spare set of hands

Screw the posts together—although not all the way—and thread them through the cuff link holes of a shirt with the stem facing out.

Open Guest Book

Use whatever shape and size frame you prefer for this tongue-in-cheek project. Determine the dimensions of the insulation needed by measuring along the inside rim on the back of the frame, also known as the rabbet.

MATERIALS

8' × 4' × ¾" sheet rigid foam insulation

Empty picture frame

12 wire brads, 1" × 18

2 heavy-duty, one-hole, D-ring picture hangers

2 picture nails

TOOLS

Utility knife

Finishing hammer

Steel measuring tape

1. Place the insulation right side up on a clean work surface. Place the frame right side up on the insulation, and tuck the tip of a pencil underneath it to trace along the inside ridge. Use a utility knife to cut out the insulation along the outline.

2. Flip the frame over so it's wrong side up and drop in the insulation, shiny side down. Secure the insulation to the frame by "toenailing" the brads into the frame. To do this, hammer the brads to the frame at a 45-degree angle to the insulation, spacing them 12" apart. If your frame is smaller, adjust your spacing accordingly.

3. To mount the hanging hardware, lay the "mirror" wrong side up on a clean surface. Measure the diameter of the frame (or the height, if you're using a square or rectangular frame) from the top edge to the bottom edge. Measure down and mark the sides of the frame about one-third the length of the diameter (or height). Mount the D-rings on the sides of the frame at the pencil marks. Measure the distance between the two D-rings. Measure and mark this distance on the wall. Mount the picture nails at the pencil marks. Slide the D-rings onto the picture nails. "Write" something on the mirror with the blunt end of a paintbrush or wooden spoon to get things started.

Drop-Dead Gorgeous Tablecloth

Denim drop cloths are not as common as the canvas and plastic varieties, but they're worth seeking out to make this very versatile cover. Like your favorite jeans, it just gets better with every spin through the washer.

MATERIALS

9' × 12' denim drop cloth (or one sized appropriately for your table), washed and dried

TOOLS

Painter's tape

Steel measuring tape

Yardstick

Sharp scissors

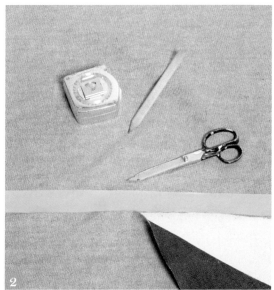

1. To determine the dimensions of your table-cloth, drape the drop cloth, dark side up, over the table. Position it so that the seams fall where you want them to—they can be centered or a bit off, depending on your preference. Mark the perimeter of the table with the painter's tape, and move the drop cloth to a clean work surface. (We used the floor.)

2. Use the steel measuring tape to measure the height of the table. Ours is 30" high. If you want the drop cloth to pool on the floor, add 2". To have it just break the floor, add 1½". To have it brush the floor, do not add any length at all. Use the measuring tape to measure and mark the cloth from the outside edge of the painters tape around all four sides. (We marked ours at 32" so that the drop cloth pools on the floor.) Use the yardstick to connect the marks with a pencil. Affix the bottom edge of the painter's tape along the marked lines and cut.

NUTS AND BOLTS
What Size Tablecloth Is the Right Size?

It depends on the look you're going for. If you want a romantic, voluptuous look, the tablecloth should pool on the floor by about 2 inches. For a more crisp, clean look, it should just hit the floor. Breaking the floor by about 1½ inches gives the table a subtle softness. Never cut a tablecloth so that the drop is less than 15 inches on all sides. Any shorter and it looks peculiar, especially if the material is a bit heavy, like denim.

Name-Dropping Wall Art

The pine boards come in 8-foot-long pieces; ask to have one cut to size right at the hardware store. You might want to play with the rope a bit before having the boards cut, though; the size of the name written in cursive may surprise you. Benjamin Moore sells small pots of paint samples that are just enough to cover small surfaces like these. The trick here is to try to "write" a name with one continuous piece of rope—it will look like rope on a board if it's cut into lots of little pieces. When nailing the rope to the board, "listen" to your rope; it will tell you where it needs to be fastened.

MATERIALS

1 quart primer

1 sample pot or ½ quart each of three different color paints in eggshell finish (we used Benjamin Moore Utah Sky/#2065-40; Benjamin Moore Sunshine/#2021-30; and Benjamin Moore Ravishing Red/#2008-10)

6" × 1" pine board, cut to lengths necessary for your children's names

20' cotton laundry line, ⅜" thick (or more, depending on the length of the names)

Steel nails, 18 gauge × 1" (figure about 50 nails per name and 25 for the "&")

2 screw eyes, ¹³⁄₁₆" each, per board

Picture wire, as needed

TOOLS

Small finishing hammer

Awl

1. Prime and paint the pine boards (see Nuts and Bolts on this page). Lightly write out the names in cursive on the right sides of the wood. You may need to do this a few times to get it right. "Write" with the rope in the same way you wrote the names out, beginning with the first letter. Nail as you go, letting the rope tell you where it needs to be nailed down. Continue around the rim. Repeat with remaining boards and names.

2. Attach the screw eyes. Measure and mark the back of each board 2" from the top and 1" from the edge on both sides. Make a pilot hole with the awl. Screw the screw eye in as far as you can with your hand. Insert the awl into the screw eye and spin it around until it is flush with the wood. Cut a length of picture wire 1" longer than the width of the board. Slide each end through each hole and twist the wire back onto itself, pulling it as taut as possible.

NUTS AND BOLTS
The Importance of Priming

It's very tempting to skip the priming step when preparing a piece of wood for paint. It may save time in the beginning, but the painted surface will never look as good—and may not take to the paint at all. Without providing paint with some "teeth," which is what primer does, the paint pools up and can even slide off.

When working with items that have a factory finish (see the Rope-Wrapped Lamp, page 86), it's essential to prime them; paint simply will not stick to these finishes.

To prepare a surface for priming, sand it first to rough it up; this will help the surface grip the primer. Primer is available in an oil-based spray, which is only used with oil-based paints, and as brush-on, which can be used with any paint.

MATERIALS

120-grit sandpaper
Spray or brush-on primer

TOOLS

All-paints paintbrush

Sand the surface and wipe it down with a soft cloth. Apply the primer and let it dry. Sand again, wipe down again, and apply your paint.

Pointillist Silhouette

Paint the canvas any color you wish. We chose this fiery treatment because it seemed more playful and less formal—perfect for the child's room where this silhouette hangs.

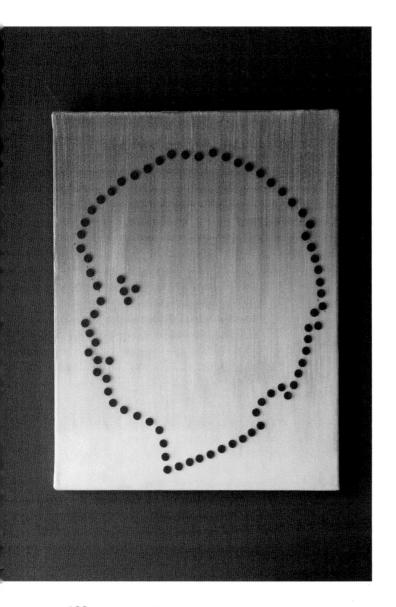

MATERIALS

Preprimed 16" × 14" stretched canvas

Tube cadmium yellow light acrylic artists' paint

Tube cadmium red acrylic artists' paint

60–80 self-adhesive sliding pads in evergreen, ⅜" each

TOOLS

1" artists' all-paints paintbrush

Steel ruler

Awl

Painter's tape

1. Place the canvas on a work surface with a short side toward you. Squeeze a quarter-size amount of yellow paint onto a piece of scrap cardboard. Place a small bowl of water next to it. Dip the brush into the water and then into the paint. Brush the yellow onto the canvas using vertical brushstrokes, going all the way from one end to the other. Let the paint dry.

2. Prepare the red paint in the same manner. Beginning at the end opposite where you started your yellow brushstrokes, brush the red paint onto the canvas. It will run out onto the yellow paint to create a moiré effect. Let the paint dry.

3. Draw the silhouette (see Nuts and Bolts below). Mark the silhouette at the tip of the nose and lips and at the center of the eyeball. Working from these points and using the steel ruler, mark the silhouette at $\frac{1}{2}$" intervals. There's a fudge factor here—you can cheat the distance a little, as long as you leave enough space between the sliding pads so that the silhouette reads nicely. Use an awl to poke through the marks on the paper.

4. Center the silhouette on the dry canvas and fasten it in place with painter's tape. Use a pencil to mark the canvas through each hole. Remove the paper silhouette and affix a sliding pad to each mark.

Nuts and Bolts
How to Draw a Silhouette

1. Tape a 17" × 14" piece of paper to a wall. If you don't have a piece that large, tape four pieces of 8½" × 11" paper together and mark and measure a 17" × 14" area on it.

2. Place the person (or dog or cat) in profile as close as possible to the piece of paper. The closer the subject is to the paper, the sharper the silhouette contours will be. (If you want to make an oversize silhouette, tape a larger piece of paper to the wall and position your subject farther from it. Remember that you'll need a larger board for a larger silhouette.) Shine a floor lamp onto the side of your subject's face, then adjust your subject's position so that his or her head fills the paper.

3. Use a pencil to trace around the silhouette projected onto the paper. To make an eye, draw a V on its side with the open part facing forward. Close up the open end with an arc to represent the eyeball.

Modernist Wall Display

We opted to see these as forms rather than as functional objects, but you can certainly use them for attractive storage.

MATERIALS

5 copper rectangular baskets, each approximately 11" × 6½" × 5¾"

10 #6 plastic anchors, 1" each

10 flat washers, $\frac{3}{16}$" each

10 #6 screws, 1" each

TOOLS

Needle-nose pliers

4-foot level

Drill with a ¼" bit

Phillips-head screwdriver

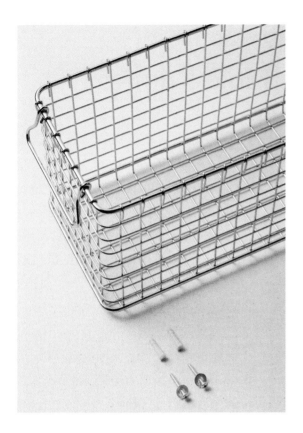

1. Use the needle-nose pliers to remove the handles from the baskets.

2. Determine where on the wall to hang the baskets; we hung ours at 6" intervals. To hang, hold the bottom basket against the wall with one hand and, using the level, make sure the basket is plumb. Use a pencil to make a mark where the inside upper left and right corners meet the wall. Drill holes in the wall at the marks. Insert a plastic anchor in each hole. Slide a washer onto a screw and screw it into the anchor. Do not tighten it all the way. If desired, paint the screw head and washer the same color as the wall. Repeat with the remaining anchors, screws, and washers.

3. Hang the baskets on the screws, then tighten the screws with the screwdriver so that the washer cinches up against the basket wire to secure it.

Arts and Crafts Table Runner

Depending on the surface you work on, the marks you make will either be shallow or deep. A hard surface, such as a stone countertop, allows for a shallow mark, whereas a softer surface—a table draped with a blanket, for example—lets you press deeper into the copper. Over time, the copper will develop a patina as it is exposed to air. If you roll it up, it will dent and kink, so store it hanging over a rod.

Unfortunately, 10-inch-wide flashing is only available in 20-foot rolls; use the extra to play with before you begin embossing your runner. Wider flashing, at 14 inches, is available in 10-foot rolls. Choose the width that is appropriate for your table.

MATERIALS

20' × 10" roll copper flashing

TOOLS

Multipurpose shears

Artist's brush or blunt-end tool

1. Use shears to cut the copper to the desired length. (We cut ours to hang just 5" over either end of the table.) Trim the corners evenly to round them out.

2. Place the copper, right side up, on a work surface covered with a sheet or drop cloth. Using the blunt end of an artist's brush, make your desired design in the copper, pressing firmly so that the design shows through to the underside. To achieve an embossed look, flip the flashing over and make marks in the remaining spaces.

5

Storage

No-Thumbtack Bulletin Board

Pegboard is typically available in 4 × 8-foot sheets; sometimes you can find smaller pieces, but if not, ask to have the sheet cut to your preferred dimensions right at the hardware store. A table saw is essential if you're going to cut it yourself and get a straight edge.

MATERIALS

2 pieces pine or stock wood,
 36" × ³⁄₄" × ³⁄₄" each

2 pieces pine or stock wood,
 17½" × ³⁄₄" × ³⁄₄" each

36" × 19" rectangle ⅛"-thick pegboard
 with ⅛" holes

10 #6 flathead wood screws, ³⁄₄" each

1 quart primer

1 quart semigloss white paint

An assortment of jumbo or extralong
 rubber bands

48 #8 flat washers (if using thin
 rubber bands)

2 screw eyes, ¹⁵⁄₁₆" each

4' picture wire

TOOLS

Wood glue

Fat-tip permanent black marker

Phillips-head screwdriver

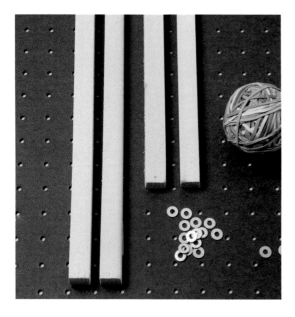

1. Use wood glue to join a long and short piece of pine together at right angles. Repeat with the remaining pieces to make a rectangular frame. Place the frame on a work surface. Color the face of the frame with a permanent black marker.

2. Apply a generous amount of wood glue around the face of the frame, then set the pegboard, right side up, on the face of the frame so that the edges are flush. Fasten the board to the frame using the ¾" flathead wood screws; place screws four holes in from each corner on every side, and one right in the center of each long side.

3. Prime and paint the pegboard and edges of the frame. Let dry.

4. To attach the rubber bands, place the pegboard face down on a work surface. Cut a rubber band and double-knot one end. Feed it through the board from the back to the front, run it along the front side, and thread it back through a hole on the opposite end of the same row of holes. Double-knot it to secure. If you are using rubber bands that are thin enough to slip through the holes even when knotted twice, thread one end with a washer and double-knot around it. Cut a second rubber band and feed it through the board from the back to the front

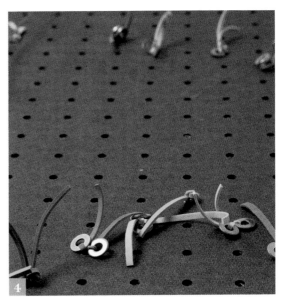

through the hole where the previous rubber band ended. Continue threading and securing the rubber bands in this manner to make concentric rectangles or to achieve your desired design.

5. To hang the bulletin board, attach the screw eyes. Measure and mark the back of the short sides of the frame, about 5" from the top. Make pilot holes with the awl. Screw the screw eyes in as far as you can with your hand. Insert the awl into the screw eye and spin it around until the screw eye is flush with the pegboard. Thread the picture wire through the screw eyes, leaving about 5" on either end. Wrap the loose ends back onto the extended wire, pulling it as taut as possible.

Foolproof Organizer

Make the cutouts any shape you like—try a circle for keys or a change purse, for example. Use a biscuit cutter or jar lid as your guide.

MATERIALS

2 cork tiles, 12" × 12" each

TOOLS

Steel ruler

Graph paper (optional)

Utility knife

Wood glue

120-grit sandpaper

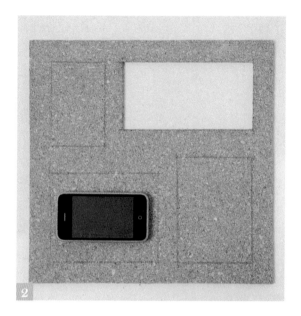

1. Arrange the items you want to organize on the cork tile. If you feel you have a steady hand and a good measuring eye, use the ruler to make boxes or circles around the items. If you prefer to be more precise, arrange your things on a piece of graph paper and outline them along the grid. Tape the graph paper to the cork tile and trace along the markings; this will make an indentation in the cork. Remove the paper and trace along the indentations with a pencil.

2. Use a very sharp utility knife to cut out the cork along the pencil lines. Set the scraps aside for another use (such as the cork switch plates shown on page 110).

3. Apply a thick line of wood glue around the cutouts on the side of the cut tile that you made the pencil marks on. Arrange the piece, glue side down, on top of the second tile so that the edges are flush. Scrape away any excess glue immediately. Place a very heavy object, such as a large book, on top of the organizer. Let the glue dry overnight.

4. Using the sandpaper, gently brush the corners to round them and give the piece a custom look.

Modular Storage

Once you begin cutting these tubes down, you'll want to start playing with their heights and widths to come up with different combinations. Of course, you can also cut them to a uniform height to achieve a more graphic look—arrange them on the floor to establish your pattern before moving it to the wall. We hung these in a narrow hallway and designated them for coats, hats, and gloves—but they would also be right at home displaying collections in a living or dining room. Refrain from stacking books, backpacks, or overstuffed book bags in them; these shelves are designed for light storage only.

The quantities of materials needed will vary depending on your design. We used about half of one 12-inch tube and the full length of a 10-inch tube.

The concrete forms are available in 10- and 12-inch diameters and are 48 inches long. Keep in mind that they are made to nest, so the sizes will vary within $\frac{3}{8}$ inch of the marked size.

MATERIALS

Assorted sizes concrete tube forms

Contact paper

#10 washers

6-32 × $\frac{1}{2}$" round combo bolts and
   nuts

3' × 4" × 1" piece of pine

1 quart primer

1 sample pot or 1 quart paint in your
   wall color

$\frac{1}{4}$" plastic anchors (10–14)

#8 sheet metal screws, 1$\frac{1}{2}$"

#6 flat brass screws, $\frac{3}{4}$"

TOOLS

Jigsaw fitted with a wood blade

Scissors

Utility knife

Awl

Drill with an $\frac{1}{8}$" bit and Phillips-head
   bit

1. Use a jigsaw to cut the concrete tube forms to your desired heights.

2. Use scissors to cut a piece of contact paper longer than the circumference of your first form and wider than that form's height. Carefully remove the adhesive backing and lay the sheet sticky side up on a work surface. Place the tube on the paper and press the paper to the tube to adhere it. Use a utility knife to cut away the excess at the top and bottom. Repeat with remaining paper and tubes.

3. Arrange the forms on the floor in your desired pattern. Where two tubes meet, mark the middle of the shallower tube with a pencil. Use an awl to poke a hole through the tubes at the pencil mark. Slide a washer onto a bolt, poke the bolt through both tubes, slide another washer onto the bolt, and secure with the nut. Fasten all of the tubes together in this way.

4. To make the shelf braces, place the shelves (the connected tubes) on the floor or on a work surface. Slide the piece of pine underneath one of the topmost tubes, making sure the top of the tube rests just below the top of the piece of pine. Trace the top arc of the interior of the tube. Make a crescent shape on the board by connecting the ends of the arc, making the center of the crescent at least 2" deep. Mark a crescent on the board for each topmost tube on the connected tube.

5. Use a jigsaw to cut out first the inside arc of each brace, followed by the outside arc. Make a pencil mark at the center of each brace and set the braces on a piece of scrap wood. Use a drill with an $\frac{1}{8}$" bit to make a pilot hole at the pencil mark, drilling completely through the piece of wood.

6. Prime and paint the braces to match your wall color so that they are barely visible.

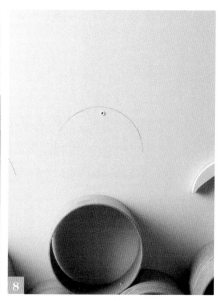

7. With the help of a friend, position the shelving on the wall where you want it to hang. Trace along the top arc of each topmost tube, marking directly on the wall. Set the shelving aside. Align the first brace with the appropriate mark on the wall. Slide the drill through the hole in the brace to drill a hole in the wall. Repeat with the remaining braces. Tap the anchors into the holes in the wall so that they are flush with the wall.

8. Align the hole in one brace with the corresponding anchor. Use the drill with a Phillips-head bit and a sheet metal screw to screw it to the wall. Repeat with the remaining braces. Set the shelving onto the braces.

9. At the back of each top tube, just above the brace, make a pilot hole with an awl. Place a brass screw in each hole and screw the shelves to the braces with the drill and Phillips-head bit.

Quick-Assembly Shelves

The uprights, called nipples, come in a range of lengths. We used the 12-inch version from top to bottom, but you can vary the lengths according to your needs (such as to work around baseboard heating). Assemble the whole thing on the floor, as if the shelves are lying on their backs, then enlist a strong friend to help you lift the assembled project into place. Because they are quite heavy, the shelves must be fastened to studs in the wall with the appropriate hardware; in our case, this meant using lead anchors because the wall is made of concrete.

MATERIALS

4 pine boards, 12" × 2" each (cut to your desired length)

20 black floor flanges, ½" each

10 black nipples, 12" × ½" each

2 black nipples, 5" × ½" each

72 #12 wood screws, ¾" each

2 elbows, ½" each

Appropriate wall anchors

TOOLS

Metal ruler

Drill with an ⅛" bit

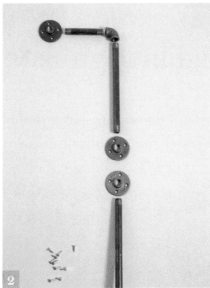

1. Place a pine board on a clean work surface. Measure and mark 2" from each end of the board, and at those marks draw lines parallel to each short edge. Mark the center of each line. Flip the board over and repeat, then do the same with the remaining three boards.

2. Thread the flanges onto the top and bottom of all but two nipples. These are your shelf supports.

3. Beginning with the underside of the bottom shelf, position one shelf support so that its outer edge touches the center mark on the parallel line. Use a pencil to mark the board through the holes in the flange. Use the $\frac{1}{8}$" bit to drill pilot holes $\frac{1}{4}$" deep at each pencil mark. Fasten the support to the board using the $\frac{3}{4}$" wood screws. Repeat on the opposite end of the board.

Center a shelf support at the center mark of one line on the top of the board. Use a pencil to mark the holes, and fasten the shelf support to the top of the board as you did in Step 2. Repeat on the opposite end.

4. Continue fastening the shelf supports below and above the boards until you reach the top side of the top shelf. Screw a flange onto one end of one of the remaining 12" nipples (this will be fastened to the board) and an elbow, followed by a 5" nipple and a flange on the other end (this will be fastened to the wall). Position the flange on the board and fasten as above. Repeat on the opposite end of the shelf.

5. With the help of a strong friend, stand the shelves upright. Set them on the wall where you want them and, using a pencil, mark the wall through the holes in the flange. Use the appropriate hardware to fasten the shelves to the wall.

See-Through Storage

With a few coats of white paint, the storage bin favored by college kids everywhere becomes a sleek white cube with a porcelainlike finish.

MATERIALS

15¾" × 12³⁄₁₆" piece Plexiglas
16½" × 13½" plastic crate
White spray paint for plastic

TOOLS

80-grit sandpaper

1. Sand the corners of the Plexiglas to round them so that they fit into the crate opening.

2. In a well-ventilated space, set the crate wrong side up. Spray paint it on all five sides. Let it dry. Flip it over and spray paint the rim and the interior. Let it dry. Spray paint one side of the Plexiglas. Let it dry. Apply as many coats of spray paint as it takes to make the pieces appear opaque. Let all of the pieces dry thoroughly.

3. Turn the crate right side up. Set the piece of Plexiglas into it with the painted side down.

6

Just Kidding

Ringtoss Redux

Mason line is a mason's best friend; it's as important to laying bricks straight as a level is when aiming for plumb surfaces. It's available in colors seemingly chosen to entice kids—hot pink, caution orange, and bright yellow. Inspired by a vintage ringtoss we spotted in an antiques store—the kind of game that charms parents but never seems to catch on with the little ones—we fashioned a brighter version. Look for a bun foot and dowel in the molding department of the hardware store.

MATERIALS

7½' nylon rope, ¾" thick

18' mason line

5" × 2¼" bun foot

12" × ½" dowel

1 quart primer

1 sample pot or 1 pint semigloss paint
(we used Benjamin Moore Utah
Sky/#2065-40)

TOOLS

Hot glue gun

Very sharp utility knife

Vise grip

Drill with a ½" bit

2" all-paints paintbrush

Wood glue

1. Plug in a hot glue gun. Cut the nylon rope into six 15" pieces. Trim both ends of each piece at a 45-degree angle, with the angle slanting in the same direction on both ends. Cover one end with hot glue, then shape the rope into a circle, lining up the ends so that they fit smoothly against one another. Hold the ends together for 30 to 60 seconds, or until the hot glue sets up. Repeat with the remaining five pieces of rope. Let dry thoroughly.

2. Cut six 3' pieces of mason line. To hide the seam (and add a colorful touch), apply a dab of hot glue on the inside of the rope circle at the seam. Place the end of one piece of mason line on the glue. Press down on it with a pencil, taking care not to push the pencil into the hot glue. When the glue has set, begin wrapping the mason line around the seam, working from left to right and back again for about 1", ending on the inside of the circle. Secure the mason line by applying a dab of hot glue on the inside of the circle on the wrapped section, and press the end of the mason line into it with a pencil. Let the glue set.

3. Use the vise grips to remove the screw on the bottom of the bun foot. Set the bun foot on a piece of scrap wood. Use a drill with a $\frac{1}{2}$" bit to drill a larger hole through the entire bun foot where the screw was.

4. Prime and paint the dowel and bun foot (see page 131). Fill the hole in the bun foot with wood glue. Slide the dowel into the hole and let the glue dry. Toss away!

Kids' Clubhouse

Roller shades can be cut to fit; to determine the size you need, measure the length and width of the table from the inside of one leg to another. The bracket size is standard, and they are typically stocked near the shades themselves. Our table leg is behind the skirt, making it easy to conceal the shades and brackets. A tack hammer allows you to get into a tight spot to install the brackets.

MATERIALS

4 roller shades cut to fit the dimensions of your table

4 pairs side mount roller shade brackets

TOOLS

Steel measuring tape

Chisel-tip permanent marker

Tack hammer

1. Measure the height of the table from the floor to the bottom edge of the tabletop. Unfurl the shades on a clean work surface, and measure and mark this height from the bottom of each shade. This is the area that will show with the shade pulled down. Sketch your clubhouse lightly in pencil first (it's easy to erase), then trace over it with the chisel-tip marker.

2. Turn the table upside down. Mount the brackets with the keyhole-shaped nail hole at the top, putting the pin bracket on the left and the slot bracket on the right. (This is the opposite of the way the shade will fall when the table is right side up.)

If your table has a skirt, set the first bracket on the leg with the top flush with the top of the table, giving it 1¼" clearance from the skirt to accommodate the thickness of the rolled-up shade. If your table doesn't have a skirt, center the bracket on the leg. Use a tack hammer to secure the bracket with the nails included in the package.

Nuts and Bolts
Determining the Width of a Roller Shade

Roller shades are measured for the total shade width, which includes the pin and the slot. This is also known as the tip-to-tip measure. Simply measure the distance between the inside edges of the legs or the apron of your table (as opposed to the width of the tabletop surface), and give that measurement to the person cutting your shades. They'll make allowances for the pin and the slot.

Royal Robot Floor Lamp

When it comes to making a robot from things you find in the hardware store, it's tempting to want to use almost everything you see. Indeed, what began as a simple little robot inspired by a childhood memory turned into the most tricked-out project in this book. Once we got started, we couldn't stop. There's no need to take things as far as we did; you can approach this project à la carte. A word of advice, however: Don't skip the doorbell. It's the part of the robot that Stephen never forgot.

The mouth gives the robot its personality—we started with a flange but thought it looked slightly menacing. By shaping a gasket into a heart, we managed to make this guy smile—an infinitely more appealing friend in the boys' bedroom.

The 12¼-inch concrete tube form will be stocked with those marked 12 inches; the width can vary by as much as a full inch within each size category. The 8⅞-inch concrete tube form will be among those marked 8 inches. Bring your tape measure to find the correct size.

MATERIALS

48" × 8⅞" concrete tube form

48" × 12¼" concrete tube form

2 rolls aluminum tape, 50 yards each

2 socket and switch sets sized for frosted lightbulbs

1 socket and switch set sized for clear tube lightbulb

Lavatory pop-up drain gasket

2 white drain grates, 4" each

12"-square piece of cardboard

2 pieces of pine, 3" × 2" × 1"

5"-square window screen

20 #6 pan head screws, 1" each

2 washers, ¼" each

2 chrome-plated plastic split flanges for ¾" pipe

2 frosted lightbulbs, 40 watts

1 clear tube lightbulb, 25 watts

Beveled tub overflow gasket

8" duct board tab collar

12" duct board tab collar

2 semirigid aluminum ducts, 4' × 3"

10 hex head bolts and nuts, 1" × ⅜" each

10 flat washers, ⅜" each

2 self-adhering LED tap lights

2½" doorbell

2 stove bolts and nuts, 8-32 × 1" each

8' bell wire

Doorbell button

15" × 1" round solid pine panel

2 gray rubber casters, 3" each

2 locking gray rubber casters, 3" each

11⅝" × 2" × 1" piece of pine

4 wood screws, 1½" long each

2 flat washers, 3/16" each

Lamp dimmer control

Power strip or three-outlet 16-gauge, 13-amp light-duty extension cord, 9' long

TOOLS

Hand saw or jigsaw

Utility knife

Hot-glue gun

One-minute, two-part epoxy

Awl

Drill with a Phillips-head bit and ⅜" bit

Pliers

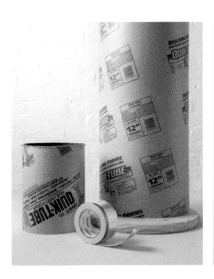

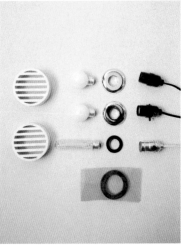

1. Cut the 48" × 8⅞" tube down to 10½" to make the head. Cut seven to nine 30" pieces of aluminum tape. Affix the tape around the tube, beginning at one end and working your way to the other, overlapping the strips as you go. Start each strip in the same place on the tube; this seam will become the back of the head.

2. With the front of the head facing you, measure and mark 3" from the top edge of the tube. Using one of the sockets as a guide, trace around it to make a circle. Measure 5" to one side and repeat to make the second circle. (These are the eyes.) Position a socket 5" from the top edge of the tube and center it 2½" from either eyehole. Trace it to make the nose. Squeeze the gasket so it's almost a heart shape, and position it 1¾" from the bottom edge of the tube and directly beneath the nose. Trace it to make the mouth. Position a drain grate so that the widest part of the grate is at least 2" from the eyehole and the top of the grate is even with the center of the eye. Trace it to make an

ear, and repeat on the other side of the head. Use a utility knife to cut out the holes for the eyes, nose, mouth, and ears. (When cutting out any holes, be conservative; you can always make them bigger to fit.)

Place the 48" × 12¼" tube on the piece of cardboard and trace around it. Cut the circle out with a utility knife. Cover the cardboard with strips of aluminum tape. Measure and mark a 1½" circle in the center of the covered cardboard and cut it out with the utility knife. Place the piece of covered cardboard right side up on a work surface. Center the robot head on it and trace around it with a pencil. Remove the head from the cardboard. Set one 3" piece of pine on the radius at 9 o'clock and the other on the radius at 3 o'clock, positioning them so that the ends are flush with the center hole. Use hot glue to attach the pine to the covered cardboard. Make a small pencil mark on the cardboard just beyond where the boards are attached to guide you when you're fastening the head to the neck.

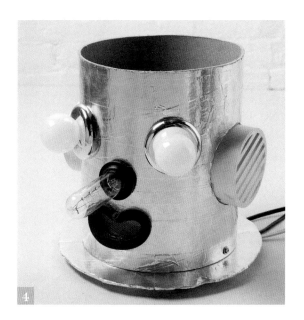

3. Working from inside the head, poke a socket for a frosted lightbulb out of each eyehole and a socket for a clear tube lightbulb out of the nose hole. Apply hot glue around the inside of the mouth. Press the screen into it and let it dry. Mix up a quarter-size quantity of epoxy. Quickly spread all of it on the back of the gasket, squeeze it into a heart shape, and affix it over the mouth hole. Hold it in place until it's thoroughly dry, about 1 minute.

Set the head onto the covered cardboard neck base, threading the cords through the center hole, and position it so that the ends of the boards are aligned with the sides of the head. Use an awl to make a pilot hole on the head in line with the pencil mark and $\frac{3}{8}$" above the bottom of the head. Use the drill with the Phillips-head bit to screw in a pan head screw threaded with a $\frac{1}{4}$" washer at each hole.

4. Thread a flange onto each of the frosted 40-watt bulbs, and screw one into each eye socket. Slide the drain gasket around the clear tube lightbulb, working it onto the bulb from its tip, and then screw the bulb into the nose socket. Pop the drain grates into the ear holes.

5. Use tin snips to trim away the 8" × 1$\frac{3}{4}$" corrugated rim of the small duct board tab collar. Set the crown into the top of the head, with the tabs sticking straight up.

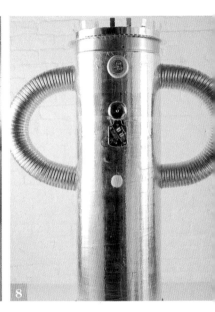

6. Cut the 48" × 12¼" concrete tube form down to 36" for the body. Cut 25 to 30 pieces of aluminum tape, each 40" long. Fasten them to the 12¼" tube using the same method as for the head (see Step 1).

To make the armholes on the body, mark the top of the tube at 3 o'clock and 9 o'clock. Mark the body 1" below these two marks for the armholes and 14½" below the marks for the hand holes. Using an aluminum duct as your template, trace the armholes and hand holes on both sides, aligning the top of the duct with each mark. Use a utility knife to cut out the four holes. Attach the arms. Fit them into the armholes and push about 4 inches of duct into the body on each end.

7. Measure and mark 2" from the bottom of the body; repeat this every 4" around the outside of the tube. Use a drill with a ⅜" bit to drill through the tube at each mark. Thread a ⅜" washer onto a hex head bolt, insert it into a hole and secure it with the nut, tightening it with the pliers. Repeat with remaining bolts and nuts.

8. Find the center front of the body. Remove the adhesive backing on one LED light and attach it to the center of the body, aligning it with the armholes. Attach the second LED light in the same way, aligning it with the hand holes. Remove the cover from the doorbell and center it between the two LED lights. Mark the two screw holes with a pencil. Use an awl to poke a hole through the body at the pencil marks. Thread the stove bolts through the bell and push them through the body. Secure on the inside with the accompanying nuts, tightening them with your hand until the bell is secure. We

 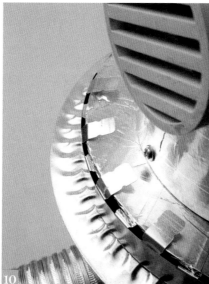 

chose not to replace the cover, but you can do so if desired. Just to the left of the terminals, use the awl to make two small holes, one on top of the other. Using the bell wire, thread the two terminal wires attached to the front through the two awl holes to the inside of the body.

9. On the 12" duct board tab collar, cut out arches to accommodate the robot's arms. Insert the large duct board tab collar, aligning the arm cutouts to fit. Push down every other tab on the collar so that they are pointed toward the center and parallel with the floor.

10. Separate the head from the neck base and set the base atop the collar on the horizontal tabs. Push the remaining tabs down onto the top of the base.

11. Bring one of the bell's terminal wires up through the hole in the neck base and thread the other through the premade hole in the base of the duct board tab collar. Set the doorbell battery onto the neck base inside the head. Hook up the bell and doorbell button according to the package directions. Place the head back onto the neck support.

12. Cut about eleven 20" pieces of aluminum tape. Fasten the tape to the top and sides of the round pine panel, starting at one side and overlapping the pieces until the circle is covered. On the wrong side of the pine panel, position the casters at 12, 3, 6, and 9 o'clock. Mark the holes with a pencil. Use an awl to make a pilot hole in each mark. Position the casters in place, with the two locking casters adjacent to each other. Use a drill with a Phillips-head bit to attach the casters to the panel with the pan head screws.

13. Lock the casters and turn the base right side up. Center the robot body on the base and trace around it with a pencil. Remove the body from the base. Set the 11⅝" × 2" × 1" pine board on the base so it spans the diameter. Mark the board 3" in from either end and use the drill to screw a 1½" wood screw into each mark. Make a pencil mark on the base just beyond where the board is positioned to guide you when fastening the body to the base.

14. Set the body onto the base, positioning it so that the ends of the board are aligned with the sides of the body. Use an awl to make pilot holes ⅜" above the bottom of the body, in line with the pencil marks. Use the drill with the Phillips-head bit to screw in a pan head screw threaded with a 3⁄16" washer at each hole.

At the very bottom of the back of the body, measure and mark a square big enough for your hand to fit through. Use the utility knife to cut out three sides, leaving the top intact. This serves as a door for the electrical cords. Pull the cords through the door. Attach the dimmer as directed on the packaging, then plug the cords into a power strip or three-outlet extension cord.

Bucket of Fun

We love the look of a clothesline hook (as pictured below), but because we weren't so keen on drilling four holes in our pressed tin ceiling, we opted for a screw hook driven

directly into a joist. If you're not mounting the hook on a joist, use a $^5/_8$-inch to $^3/_4$-inch drywall anchor. Insert it using a drill with a $^5/_{16}$-inch bit, and use an $^1/_8$-inch screw eye for the hook.

MATERIALS

Empty 1-gallon paint can with lid

Multicolor adhesive letters

#8 × 2$^9/_{16}$" hook or $^5/_{16}$" zinc-plated clothesline hook

20' twisted nylon rope, $^1/_2$" thick

2" fixed single pulley

TOOLS

Drill with a $^5/_{16}$" bit (if using an anchor)

1. Decide what phrase you want on your bucket, and firmly adhere the appropriate letters to the empty paint can.

2. Screw or mount the hook to a joist in the ceiling. (If you're using an anchor, see the instructions at top.) Thread one end of the rope through the pulley and tie it off in a double-knot. Tie the other end of the rope to the bucket handle and tie it off in a double-knot.

Quiet Cannon

Though 1 × 10-inch boards are typically sold in 6-foot lengths, you really only need to cut a circle with a 7½-inch diameter. Before buying a whole board, ask your friendly hardware store owner if there are any scraps that fit your needs. The same goes for the 2 × 3-inch pine, which only comes in 8-foot lengths. Keep in mind that building forms are designed to telescope, so those labeled 8 inches in diameter can actually range in size. Bring along your tape measure to be sure you're getting the size you need.

MATERIALS

3" × 2" piece of pine

48" × 8" concrete tube form

6 #8 pan head screws, 1" each

2 #8 flat washers

10" × 1" pine board, or a scrap at least 10" × 8" × 1"

5"-long finial

1 can (13 ounces) spray primer

Matte black spray paint

1½" dowel, 15" long

⁷⁄₁₆" dowel, 12" long

2 round solid pine pieces, 18" diameter each

Wood stain

1 6" cotton rope, ¼" thick, knotted on one end

2 pipe straps, 1¼" each

TOOLS

Awl

Drill with Phillips-head, $\frac{1}{4}$", $\frac{7}{64}$", $\frac{3}{8}$", and $\frac{1}{2}$" spade bits

Utility knife

Compass

Jigsaw

Pliers

60-grit sandpaper

Wood glue

1. Trim the 3" × 2" pine to 24" long. Measure and mark the outside of the building form 3" from the top edge and then 10" below that. Use an awl to make holes in the form at the pencil marks. On the inside of the form, measure and mark $\frac{3}{4}$" from the edge, above the top hole. Directly opposite these marks, mark the form $3\frac{1}{2}$" from the top edge on the inside of the form.

2. Thread a washer onto each of two screws. Slide the 24" × 3" × 2" piece of pine into the form up against the holes. The top should be aligned with the inside pencil mark. Use the drill and the Phillips-head bit to fasten the board to the form with the screws. Use your free hand to hold the board in place and to apply pressure. Use a drill with a $\frac{1}{4}$" bit to make a hole at the mark opposite.

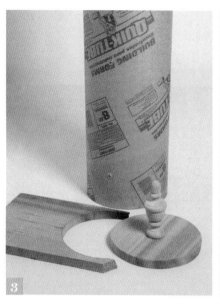

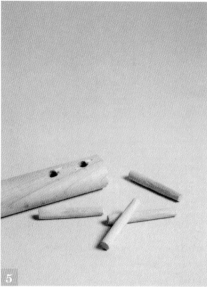

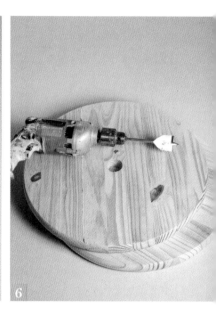

3. Measure the inner diameter of the concrete form. (Ours is 7½".) Use a compass to draw a circle the correct diameter on the 10" × 1" board or scrap piece. Use a jigsaw to cut out the circle. Use a drill with a 7/64" bit to make a ¼"-deep pilot hole in the center of the circle. Screw the finial into the hole.

4. Prime and paint the concrete tube form and the end piece with the finial, and set them aside to dry.

5. Measure and mark the 1½"-thick dowel 1" and 2⅜" from one end. Repeat at the other end. Lay the dowel on its side on a piece of scrap wood with the pencil marks facing you. Use a drill with a ⅜" bit to drill through the dowel at each of the four pencil marks.

Cut the 7/16" dowel into four 3" pieces, and make a pencil mark 1½" from one end of each piece. Use a utility knife to whittle the pieces down, tapering them slightly from the 1½" mark until one end is 5/16" in diameter to make pins for the wheels.

6. Place one 18" pine round on a piece of scrap wood. Use a 1½" spade bit to drill through the center of the round, using the dimple in the center as a guide. Repeat with the second round.

7. Apply the stain to the wheels and all dowels with a rag. (You may want to wear latex gloves to do this.). Let them dry overnight. Slide a pin into each of the two innermost holes on the axle. Slide a wheel onto each end and secure with a second pin on the outside of each wheel. Tap the pins into the holes until they're tight.

8. Put the knotted rope inside the cannon and use a pair of pliers to pull it through the hole at the top of the cannon. Put the cap into the open hole in the cannon body closest to the fuse. If it doesn't fit, sand it down with 60-grit sandpaper. When it fits well, apply a thick layer of wood glue around the rim and fit the end piece into the top of the cannon. Let the glue dry.

9. Measure and mark the body 17½" from the back of the cannon, directly below the existing screws. Measure and mark the body ⅜" on either side of this mark. Working with one strap at a time, position one end of the pipe strap at each mark. Mark the top and bottom holes with a pencil. Use an awl to make a hole at each mark. Use the drill with the Phillips-head bit and the pan head screws to fasten only the tops of the straps to the body. Attach the wheels under the straps by bending them back to slide the axle into them. Fasten the loose ends to the body as above. Fire away!

Snap-On Suit of Armor

We used ½-inch-thick Reflectix insulation, which is easy to cut and shape around little arms and legs.

MATERIALS

25' × 16" roll reflective insulation

Industrial strength adhesive-backed Velcro, 4' × 2" strip

48" × 8" concrete tube form

50-yard roll aluminum tape

Large piece of newspaper or kraft paper

12"-square piece foam core board

4' × ¾" dowel

TOOLS

Scissors

Utility knife

Handsaw or jigsaw

Black permanent marker

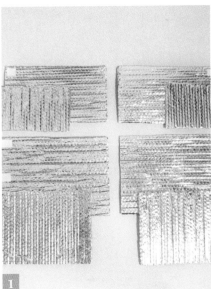

1. Measure the length of the child's forearm from wrist to elbow. Measure the width of his forearm around the thickest part, and add 1½" to that measurement. Cut two pieces of insulation to these dimensions.

Measure and cut two pieces of insulation for the upper arms, lower legs, and thighs in the same manner.

2. Fold the insulation in half so that you have two layers of insulation that are slightly longer than your child's torso. Use one of the child's shirts as a pattern, aligning the shoulders on the fold and cutting away at the armholes. Trace around the shirt with the marker, then cut out along the lines, leaving the shoulders uncut.

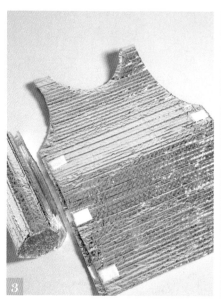

3. Cut 22 squares of Velcro, 2" × 2" each. Affix one piece to each end of each piece of arm and leg armor, and place three pieces, equidistant apart, on both sides of the body armor.

4. Use the utility knife to cut the building form on the diagonal, with the higher end coming to a point. Beneath the pointed tip, cut an opening in a thick U shape for the eyes. Adhere the aluminum foil tape to the helmet.

5. Fold a piece of newspaper or kraft paper in half. Draw an axe head on the fold and cut it out. Unfold and use it as the pattern for the battle-axe. Place the pattern on the foam core board and trace it with a pencil. Cut out the battle-axe with the utility knife. Adhere the aluminum foil tape to the axe head.

6. Use a handsaw or jigsaw to cut a 2"-long slice down the center of one end of the dowel. Slide the axe head into it.

ACKNOWLEDGMENTS

First off, I must thank my phenomenal husband whose talent amazes me every single day. Collaborating with him is a joy and a privilege that I never take for granted. A big round of applause goes to our two boys, Finn and James, who turn every trip to the hardware store into a treasure hunt. Or a game of hide and seek.

We have both worked with dozens of wonderful photographers over the years, but among them, Lesley Unruh is a photographer *de rêve*. Not only did she unblinkingly cut the tips of her knit gloves so that she could click the camera in Stephen's quasi-heated studio, but she lent that rare combination of style, professionalism, and grace to the project. She also brought a delightful and multitalented assistant in Jada Vogt, whose sense of humor never failed us. It was just the four of us—and it was never so much fun to go to work.

A heartfelt thank-you to neighbors and friends who graciously loaned us their homes—and everything in them—in which to take the pictures. Tad Hills and Lee Wade and their remarkably talented children Elinor and Charlie (that's one of his pillow designs on pages 12 and 90) let us into their charming home more than once. Chris Sheller gave us the keys to his loft and allowed us to move everything around in his space. Al McGowan and Hilary Robertson and the adorable Gus (that's his art work on pages 13 and 93) gave us full run of their prop-filled apartment for several days, an above-and-beyond gesture of kindness. We are indebted to Kara Hamilton for sharing her upstate New York home and studio, an inspired place to say the least. Steve Marks and Cate Springer came through when we had exhausted every nook and cranny in our own home.

It's one thing to design things, photograph them, and write about them, but it's another to have the full confidence in a publisher who will turn it into a wonderful book. Pam Krauss has been doing it successfully for years and we are proud to be among her authors. Editor Denise McGann handled so many moving parts with good humor and designer Chris Gaugler put them all together beautifully. Thank you to you both for working so tirelessly. Copyediting a book filled with hundreds of nut, bolt, and screw sizes, projects with multiple steps, and images that must match up to instructions is nothing short of a Herculean task. We owe a debt of gratitude to Erana Bumbardatore and Paula Brisco for doing the math every time. Editorial assistant Victoria Glerum became our go-to gal when the book was in the home stretch; she picked up all of the pieces with aplomb. Project editor Nancy Bailey kept the manuscript moving.

Many thanks to our agent, Angela Miller, whose love of hardware stores prompted that question all would-be authors want to hear from their agents, "Why don't you. . . ?" Her fab colleagues Sharon Bowers and Jennifer Griffin provided thoughtful suggestions during the proposal stage.

We could fill a book with the names of family, friends, and colleagues who always seem to surface when we need them most. Thank you all for your much appreciated support and enthusiasm. Linda Kocur, in particular, provided valued design inspiration at the outset. Namrata Pradhan gave our boys undivided attention whenever we needed her throughout this project and for the past seven years. We hope that you take as much pleasure in the following pages as we did in creating them.

Stephen Antonson and Kathleen Hackett,
New York City, 2010

INDEX

Boldface page references indicate photographs. Underscored references indicate boxed text.